Lermontov's
A Hero of Our Time

Robert Reid

Bristol Classical Press
Critical Studies in Russian Literature

For Anne Reid with thanks
for patient preparation of the typescript

First published in 1997 by
Bristol Classical Press
an imprint of
Gerald Duckworth & Co. Ltd
61 Frith Street
London W1D 3JL
e-mail: inquiries@duckworth-publishers.co.uk
Website: www.ducknet.co.uk

Reprinted (with minor additions) 2001

A catalogue record for this book is available
from the British Library

ISBN 1-85399-424-3

Printed in Great Britain by
Antony Rowe Ltd, Eastbourne

Contents

Introduction

Mikhail Lermontov's *A Hero of Our Time* (1840) is one of the great landmarks of Russian nineteenth-century prose. Together with Pushkin's *Eugene Onegin* (1830) and Gogol's *Dead Souls* (1842) it set the aesthetic, psychological and sociological precedents on which subsequent exponents of Russian realism, Turgenev, Tolstoy, Dostoevsky and Chekhov would draw. Despite its undoubted influence on successive novels *A Hero of Our Time* has a unique and complex structure which has defied imitation. It is a novel skilfully wrought out of five interlinking stories which are held together thematically by a Byronic hero, Grigory Pechorin, and formally by an ingeniously contrived and enigmatic itinerant narrator who, touring the Caucasus during the 1830s, learns of Pechorin both from hearsay and from his journal which he fortuitously acquires and which supplies much of the novel itself.

Lermontov, who died in a duel aged twenty-seven in 1841, was primarily a poet and one moreover deeply influenced by Byronic Romanticism. His prose output is small and *A Hero of Our Time* is in many ways a 'poet's novel' in which the lyric principle, evidenced by the sacrifice of plot in favour of subjective expression, generally prevails. However, Lermontov had another reason for structuring his novel in a manner which concealed the conventional fictional techniques of his contemporaries. He wished to distance himself from the suggestion, easier to make in the case of his poetry, that the hero of his novel was but a thinly disguised self-portrait. By setting up a complex system of multiple narrators he was able to objectify his work to such a degree that it was not, to some contemporary readers at least, self-evidently a novel at all, but rather a travelogue. Early translators, in particular, seem to have assumed that it was a genuine account of travels in the Caucasus. Nevertheless some contemporary critics were quick to level the accusation of autobiographical self-portraiture at the author, a point about which he was sufficiently sensitive that he added to the second edition of the work an expostulatory preface; this, being now generally accepted as an integral part of the novel proper, has itself contributed to the latter's structural complexity.

The mainstream of Russian criticism, however, was not slow to grasp that in Pechorin Lermontov had provided a penetrating portrayal of a 'superfluous man', a typically disillusioned and embittered young Russian aristocrat of the post-Decembrist period. Stifled by social and political restrictions, he vents his frustrations on the unfortunate representatives of convention with a creative ingenuity which, in other times and circumstances, might have found a less destructive expression. More recent criticism has been fascinated by the novel's style and structure, its multiple ironies and resistance to closure, which make it amenable to both structuralist and, in our own time, post-structuralist analysis.

The present study is written in the wake of several important modern monographs in English particularly those of Turner, Gilroy and Barratt and Briggs. I have sought to acquaint the reader with these and other commentators in the course of my study but have also attempted to highlight and explore more neglected aspects of the novel: the Caucasian dimension; the relation of *Bela* to *Maxim Maximych*; the anonymity of the hero in *Taman*; the structure of *Princess Mary*, particularly the implications of diary form; the ludic impulses which inform a number of Pechorin's activities from duelling to verbal repartee and have a particular relevance to *The Fatalist*. My approach has been straightforward: Chapter 1 explores the creative and critical history of the novel; Chapters 2 to 6 analyse the constituent stories of the novel in turn, while Chapter 7 considers together the Preface to the novel and the Foreword to Pechorin's Journal. In general I have read the stories (to adapt Turner's terminology) both *autotelically* and *heterotelically*: as both free-standing texts and as parts of the organic whole of the novel. In this way it is hoped that, while dealing with the often intricate fabric of each story, the overall architecture of the novel will never be far from view. Quotations from the novel are taken from the Penguin edition, translated by Paul Foote, unless otherwise stated, and all references to critical works in the text relate to the bibliography of secondary sources at the end of the study. The transliteration system is Library of Congress minus diacritics, except in the case of surnames with 'established' forms in English (e.g. Tolstoy for Tolstoi).

Creative and Critical Context

1. Creative History

The creative history of *A Hero of Our Time* is complex in accordance with the complexity of its structure, for some of the individual stories which comprise the novel were published before the novel itself. *Bela*, *The Fatalist*, and *Taman* were all published separately in the *Otechestvennye zapiski* journal between 1839 and 1840. The idea of combining them into a novel seems to have occurred to Lermontov in 1838 and some authorities maintain that *Taman* was written a year earlier without, therefore, any intention by Lermontov of including it in the novel. Early drafts of the novel identify the narrator of the Journal as a travelling army officer, but this identification disappears in the published version. Even in its earliest drafts the work was in two parts, the first (the officer's notes) comprising *Bela* and *Maxim Maximych*, the second consisting of Pechorin's Journal which at first contained only *Princess Mary*; in 1839, still in draft form, *The Fatalist* was added to the Journal in the position now occupied by *Taman*. At this time a provisional title was added to the whole novel: 'One of the heroes of the beginning of the century' a curious formulation which gives some ground for suspecting that Pechorin was originally conceived as a Decembrist. The final version, which was published in April 1840 added *Taman* to the collection with *The Fatalist* relegated to the terminal position. Lermontov also added the introduction to Pechorin's Journal between *Maxim Maximych* and *Taman*.

The principal structural elements of the novel were thus all in place by the publication of the first edition in 1840: 1) *Bela*; 2) *Maxim Maximych*; 3) The Introduction to Pechorin's Journal; 4) *Taman*; 5) *Princess Mary*; 6) *The Fatalist*; the title was now *Geroi Nashego Vremeni*. In 1841, however, a second edition of the novel came out and Lermontov took this opportunity to insert an author's preface before *Bela* as a riposte to the sharp criticism to which the first edition had been subjected in some quarters. As a recent commentator notes, this preface has come to be treated as part of the text (Cornwell, 1995: xvi), but, as we shall see later, its incorporation is problematic. Another alteration made for the second edition was the division of the whole novel into two parts, Part Two beginning with *Princess Mary*. Since this division cuts Pechorin's Journal in two, consigning *Taman* to Part One, along with *Bela* and *Maxim Maximych*, it has sometimes figured prominently in structural criticisms of the novel.[1] However, it is now more generally accepted that the division was made for the pragmatic editorial purpose of dividing the novel as near as possible into two equal halves.

All of the stories deal with the hero, Pechorin's, sojourn in the Caucasus, as an army officer, probably around 1830. There are hints in the novel that he has been posted there for some misdemeanor in the capital. On his way to the Caucasus he stops at the town of Taman in the Crimea, so that the story of that name is chronologically, but not expositionally, the first. The next story in sequential terms is *Princess Mary*, the fictional year of which Nabokov fixes at 1832. According to one commentator we must fill up the intervening two years with Pechorin's campaigning against insurgent tribesmen, the sojourn at Piatigorsk being part of an official leave (Richards, 1994:x1). The duel with Grushnitsky results in Pechorin's being exiled to the fort, in Chechnya, north-east Caucasus, where the incident described in *Bela* takes place. The area is only doubtfully under Russian control and in the Caucasian hinterland resistance to Russian imperial encroachment by Muslim tribesmen is intense (even the spa town of Piatigorsk, the location of *Princess Mary*, is not immune from attack by Circassian *abreks* [guerrillas]). There is some disagreement as to whether *The Fatalist* post- or pre-dates the 'Bela' incident. The latter seems more likely: while at the fort in Chechnya Pechorin spends a fortnight at a Cossack settlement where the 'Fatalist' incident takes place. After Bela's death Pechorin leaves the army to travel. *Maxim Maximych* comes later still; it is five years after the 'Bela' incident (1837 according to Nabokov's chronology [Nabokov, 1984:ix]) that the Narrator and Maxim Maximych encounter Pechorin in Vladikavkaz on his way to Persia.[2] Some time after this the Narrator hears that Pechorin has died on his way back from Persia and decides to publish his notes. The foreword to the Journal, then, is the chronologically final part of the text proper, although, as already noted, the Author's Preface was added later still for the novel's second edition.

Literary influences on the novel can be divided into two categories: those which appear to have provided some precedent or inspiration for the novel as a whole, and those which can be detected in particular sections or thematic elements of it. Certain non-Russian works are clearly crucial; among these are Benjamin Constant's *Adolphe* (1816) and de Musset's *Confession d'un Enfant du Siècle* (1836) both of which feature introspective character analysis and confession. Marlinsky's tales of the Caucasus had been eagerly read by Lermontov and he would surely have known that his own work would be read in the context of the works of this enormously popular writer. Pushkin's pioneering works on the Caucasus, particularly *The Caucasian Captive* and *Journey to Arzrum* are evident in the plot of *Bela* and the travel notes respectively, while the influence of Pushkin is also detectable at specific points in the work: Maxim Maximych is sometimes compared to Samson Vyrin of *The Station Master* and the creation of atmosphere in *Taman* to that in *The Undertaker* (see Meyer, 1992:68-9). Some critics find echoes of *The Gipsies* in *Taman*, the smugglers having affinities to the travelling people in Pushkin's poem (Gifford, 1950:113); and many comparisons have been made with *Eugene Onegin*, particularly between the hero and Pechorin himself and between the protagonists of *Princess Mary* and those of Pushkin's novel.

The question of influence, however, is not easily divorced from that of critical partiality or ideology and we shall find that the question of literary influence, particularly the nature and degree of it, has become an important ingredient in recent attempts to canonically reappraise Lermontov and his novel.

2. Critical History

Few would dispute that *A Hero of Our Time* is one of the major Russian novels of the nineteenth century. Mersereau (1962:157) sees it as absolutely crucial to the future development of the Russian novel: 'At one moment Lermontov transformed the Russian novel from its embryonic state into a refined and mature art-form, not only setting the standard for later novelists but opening to them the area of their future mastery, psychological realism'. Precisely why the novel came to establish itself in such a position is a question which has occupied critics over the last hundred and fifty years. Jean Bonamour (1987; 408) may come close to the point when he suggests that the generality of its title (its non-eponymous 'Hero') is a clue to its key position in the complex intertextual nexus which links the mature novels of Turgenev, Tolstoy and Dostoevsky to the works of Karamzin, Pushkin and Gogol: in *A Hero of Our Time* the problematic of creating a literary hero was foregrounded and generalised.

The canonical status of the novel, however, has not been proof against the ebb and flow of critical sympathy both for the work itself, its hero, and indeed its creator. Critical attitudes to Lermontov's novel polarised immediately after publication. As is well known, Nicholas I quite liked it until he realised that its hero was not to be Maxim Maximych as he had hoped. This reaction was in fact also reflected in the negative reception of the novel by contemporary Slavophile or nationalist critics such as Shevyryov and Apollon Grigoriev for whom, as Ellen Chances points out, Maxim *was* the hero (Chances, 1978: 40-1). Shevyryov complained that the negative features of Pechorin's character were largely western in origin and if he is 'a hero of our time' then he is a hero for the west, not for Russia (Shevyryov, 1967: 301). Furthermore, argued Shevyryov, of all the characters in the novel, he is the most unreal because he reflects western not Russian ideas. Pechorin thus stepped straight into the dominant philosophical argument of the age in Russia between Slavophiles and Westernisers, and, from the Slavophile point of view, fell short because he did not exhibit the requisite features of Russian nationality, a central condition of the Slavophile literary aesthetic. By contrast, Belinsky attempted to establish the actuality of the novel's hero by insisting that those who refuse to regard him as typical of his time were simply being hypocritical; he also established the importance of Pechorin as a literary character by exploring his contrasts and affinities to Pushkin's

Eugene Onegin, in this launching a fruitful critical tradition which we will explore later in this work particularly in the context of *Princess Mary*.

The subsequent development of criticism of the novel in the nineteenth century was neatly summed up by G.Fedders at the beginning of our own: 'In the sixties (criticism) dethroned Pechorin and in the nineties it put him on a pedestal' (Fedders, 1914:137). The heirs of Belinsky – Pisarev, Zaitsev and, particularly, Dobrolyubov – criticised Pechorin for his aimlessness and lack of action; in fact we can say that Pechorin had been retrospectively devalued for these critics by his successors in the role of literary hero, particularly by Goncharov's Oblomov who was regarded, rightly, as the epitome of inactivity and slothfulness. However, in the seventies and eighties Apollon Grigoriev and Dostoevsky began to bring about a new attitude to Pechorin by stressing the demonic characteristics of his character as something characteristically Russian (see Usok, 1981:49-94). Grigoriev saw in Pechorin an anticipation of Stavrogin, Dostoevsky's most 'demonic' character, perhaps, and Dostoevsky himself was drawn to the combination in Pechorin of aspects of both self-deification and self-denigration, a combination which, far from paralysing his will, urged him to activity (see Belov, 1975:130). This complex of impulses can be detected in several of Dostoevsky's characters. Towards the end of the century and beyond there took place a general reappraisal of Lermontov's whole work in accordance with the symbolism, mysticism and theologism ushered in by the fin de siècle. Further emphasis was laid on the demonic, split and paradoxical nature of Lermontov's characters, and of Lermontov himself: Nietzschian traits were detected (see Merezhkovsky, 1972). Vladimir Solovyov highlighted the theme of revolt against divine order.

For ideological reasons the principal project of Soviet literature was to show that *A Hero of Our Time* was essentially a realist novel despite the fact that practically everything else its author had written had been uncompromisingly romantic. If it was a realist novel it could be portrayed historically in broadly reductionist terms which defined it as symptomatic of the period of disillusionment which followed on the failure of the Decembrist revolt under the repressive regime of Nicholas I. According to this critique Pechorin accurately typified the depressed spirit of the age. Inevitably Soviet criticism leaned heavily on the authority of Belinsky whose view of Pechorin as accurately reflecting a contemporary type supported the official modern view. Two things, however, prevented this reading from thoroughly establishing itself in Russia during the Soviet period. One was the determination of certain critics, Fokht, for instance, to address the problem of Lermontov's romanticism; another was the legacy of Eikhenbaum's Formalist criticism of the novel which urged examination of its complex structure as an alternative key to its creative excellence. William Todd is therefore not covering all the ground when he claims that the history of the reception of *A Hero of Our Time* can 'be outlined according to the critics' emphasis on the relative value of "hero" or "time"' (Todd, 1986:162). This certainly epitomises the two principal approaches to the hero, but the novel itself also attracts a third avenue of interpretation, the one which is probably the most dominant at the present time, that of 'structure'.

3.   Structure

Shevyryov, despite his very negative reception of the novel when it was first published, was also responsible for perhaps the earliest, albeit inadvertent, tribute to the novel's structural ingenuity: 'All events, all characters and details, stick to the hero of the story, Pechorin, as threads of a spider's web, laden with bright winged insects, stick to a huge spider which has entrapped them in its net' (Shevyryov, [1841] 1967:300-2). This model, though perhaps biased towards character at the expense of structure, is all the more remarkable for the fact that it was by no means universally obvious to the early readership that *A Hero of Our Time* should be regarded as a novel at all, particularly given the fact that some of its components had been published as separate entities in their own right (see Boyd, 1972:29-30). Evidence of uncertainty about the work's organic status may readily be gleaned from early translations (Reid, 1986[a]:passim). However we get no strong sense of an interest in the novel's structure *per se* in the criticism until the advent of Formalism and Eikhenbaum's detailed research into the subject. Ironically Eikhenbaum's method was to deconstruct the very notion of the work as a novel which had grown up unreflectingly in the years since its publication. He began from the position that *A Hero of Our Time* was neither a collection of tales nor a novel, but rather travel notes with a journal attached to them. Since, as Mersereau points out (Mersereau, 1983:310), travel notes were passé as a genre by Lermontov's time and none of the genres in the Journal were without precedent elsewhere, Lermontov's innovation lay in his combination of the two. Eikhenbaum's thesis is that Lermontov's adherence to the narratorial primacy of the travel notes necessitates the implementation of ingenious devices to 'motivate' the illusion that we are indeed reading travel notes and not a staightforward fictional narrative. He also points out that *A Hero of Our Time* improves on the popular tale cycle (e.g. *The Tales of Belkin*) of the 1830s, in which a number of stories with different heroes were attributed to the hand of a single fictitious narrator or collector (Eikhenbaum, 1981: 163-4). Lermontov's innovation is to give all his tales a single hero and yet, since the dominant narratorial medium is that of the travel notes, the order of the events which comprise the novel's plot is not, as more traditionally, determined by the hero but by the narrator of the notes. What Eikhenbaum reveals is an organised hierarchy of narration which later critics, partly under the influence of Bakhtinian ideas, will translate into a system of polyphony or multiple voicing.

Another Formalist preoccupation, that of the distinction between *fabula* and *sujet*, has been adapted in recent years to investigate the nature of the organic relationship between Journal and travel notes. Gregg, for instance, argues that the *sujet* (text order) of the novel has been unnecessarily privileged at the expense of the *fabula* (the presumed 'real order' of events outlined above [Gregg, 1984:387]). This has led to a general acceptance of the fact that Pechorin is not a chronologised figure, since we encounter him not via the sequential passage of time, but according to the scheme dictated by the dominant travel note structure of the novel. Todd, too, argues that the text order 'obscures Pechorin's becoming' (Todd, 1986:149) although this process can be reconstructed by considering the stories in their historical order. Not all critics agree with this point of view however: Gerstein maintains that to unravel the novel in this way is not legitimate since Lermontov clearly wished it to be dehistoricised (Gerstein, 1976:33). Ripp argues convincingly that Lermontov deliberately wrote the novel in reaction to the regnant historicism of his time and to the historical novel in particular the linear principle of which it explodes (Ripp, 1977:978). Indeed, many structural critics are prepared to go further, seeing the structure as a calculated device aimed at creating ambiguity and lack of closure. This approach seems to be primarily western, and a recent one at that, though, among Soviet critics, Grigoryan argued that the novel's apparent progression towards a greater intimacy with its hero is in fact illusory since his portrait remains vague and inconclusive (Grigoryan, 1975:209-10).

We find this idea taken to its extreme conclusion in the work of Gilroy who, taking a post-structuralist and strongly receptionist line, sees Lermontov involved in a wilful act of lectorial disorientation in the novel, as he abandons the reader to his/her own conclusions, much as God abandons humankind to its fate (Gilroy, 1989:28). However, Gilroy conceives reading, in the manner of Derrida and Huizinga, as play: an open reading of the novel reveals its depths of irony, a trope which is, for Gilroy, the dominant stylistic feature of the work; indeed it is the *raison d'être* (Gilroy, 1989:4 and 41). To read for meaning is to obscure the irony. The construction of reader interest as play puts Gilroy's approach totally at odds with traditional views of the novel like those of I. Vinogradov: that reader interest is maintained by the novel's gradual revelation of Pechorin's character (Vinogradov, 1969: 157). Paradoxically Gilroy's approach deals with structure by declining to address it since, if to discuss structure is to discuss meaning, and we are not meant to read for meaning, we will not be able to discuss structure except as a device aimed at resisting lectorial closure. Other critics however (Bagby [1978], Aizlewood [1990], Barratt and Briggs [1989], Sollertinsky [1973]) approach the phenomenon of structure via the less anarchic means of Bakhtinian polyphony or dialogism and, indeed, the work's multi-voicing or, as Milner-Gulland calls it 'multiple ambiguity of message' (Milner-Gulland, 1979:126) is clearly one of its principal structural foundations.

Finally a line of approach to the same phenomenon which perhaps merits further exploration is that advanced by Markovich: the link between openness of interpretation and structural incompleteness (Markovich, 1993). *A Hero of*

Our Time is indeed incomplete in the sense that its author left himself scope to continue or amplify Pechorin's Journal by implying in its introduction that the Narrator intended to publish separately those of Pechorin's notes which he had not included in *A Hero of Our Time*. As Waszink points out 'unfinished-ness, inconclusiveness or fragmentariness are central to romantic aesthetics in its revolt against classicism's aesthetics of perfection' (Waszink, 1990:311).

4. The Hero

Much discussion of *A Hero of Our Time* has centred, of course, not on the structure of the novel but on its hero. Indeed it is hard to make a clear separation in this case between the history of the novel's reception and that of its hero. Nevertheless there are some characterological approaches which deserve mention. Many analysts of Pechorin's character see him as a split or divided personality, because, in his passages of self-revelation (most of which are in *Princess Mary*) he himself alludes to such inner divisions as the heart and the head, the dead part of the self and the living etc. Of all these characterisational dichotomies that between fate and free will has been the most fully discussed, since it seems to offer the possibility of synthesising an explanation for the hero's actions with a rational account of his character. Recently feminist criticism has turned its attention to Pechorin and one critic in particular, Barbara Heldt, has transformed the question of Pechorin's fatedness by asking whether Pechorin 'is fated... to be fatal to women' (Heldt, 1987:31). On the whole, and not surprisingly, Pechorin is not treated leniently by feminist critics. Andrew concludes that 'the novel *as a whole*, and not simply Pechorin's character and his treatment of women, is a deeply misogynistic account of the female (and, specifically, the feminine) character' (Andrew, 1988:53). Attempts to psycho-analyse Pechorin have also been undertaken: Barratt and Briggs with the aid of Jungian psychology (they diagnose 'persona inflation' as his problem [Barratt and Briggs, 1989:67]) and by Axelrod who attributes his 'unfortunate character' and misogyny to mother-loss (Axelrod, 1993:115). For Andrew Pechorin is 'Sadeian man par excellence' (Andrew, 1988:69); Pozov considers him a sado-masochist (Pozov, 1975:106) and Hansen-Love (1993: 426ff) hints at possible homo-erotic motifs. Harkins identifies his problem with that of the modern existential hero (1964:204).

In general, however, post-modernist conventions of recent years suggest approaches to character which do not lose sight of textuality and fictionality. Both Turner and Gilroy stress the fact that Pechorin's confessions are so contextualised as to throw doubt on the truth they purport to reveal. Turner indeed speculates that the vagueness and stylisation of the confessions recalls the tone of introspection found in Lermontov's lyric verse (*Duma* being a popular paradigm among critics) an affinity which again throws doubt on the literal status of these passages (Turner, 1978:30). The contradictory views expressed by Pechorin in his confessions should not be regarded as problematic, however, because they are deliberately formulated in this way according to romantic convention (Rosenshield, 1988:97): the romantic writer articulates his own ambivalence through the mouth of his fictional creation. We may also have to accept that some of the inconsistencies in Pechorin's character arise from the fact that the stories which reveal his actions and thoughts were originally conceived independently of each other (in the case of *Taman* without reference to Pechorin it is often argued [Rosenshield, 1988:97]).

On the whole, then, although there have been many critics ready to assume with Efremov that Pechorin's Journal 'frankly records his thoughts feelings and impressions' (Efremov, 1966: 118) recent developments in Lermontov criticism point to the necessity of viewing such elements far more cautiously in favour of a more holistic approach to the novel.

5.   Detractors

This is perhaps not too harsh a heading under which to consider those critics who have tried to argue that some of the more enigmatic features of *A Hero of Our Time* are related to the youthfulness of its author. This view has a strong champion in Nabokov whose annotated translation of *A Hero of Our Time* is notable for its stylistic criticisms of the novel. Warner detects in this a kind of Bloomian project on Nabokov's part to transcend his predecessor (Warner, 1986).[3] Garrard (1981:46) is more explicit, however, when he points out the fact that *A Hero of Our Time* is a young man's book and he contrasts the novel's inner characterisation techniques unfavourably with those of Tolstoy.

Another negative critique of the novel centres on the view that it is intertextually over-determined, that its theme and technique are not as original as is commonly thought. In a qualified form this view was not unknown in Soviet criticism, Gorelov, for instance, suggesting that it was not the themes of *A Hero of Our Time* which were original but rather the extreme cynicism of its hero (Gorelov, 1964:80-1). Wolf Schmid recently attempted a comprehensive intertextual 'account' of the novel in terms of a combination of various precedents, particularly the Rousseauan confession and the Byronic poem, specifically in its ironic and demonic aspects (Schmid, 1993).

However, some features of the novel, such as eavesdropping, criticised from Nabokov onwards for its obtrusiveness, may have a functional justification or, in Eikhenbaumian terms, motivation, in the context as a whole. Thus although the instances of eavesdropping clearly are devices for securing information crucial in a first person narrative, they also serve a positive role at the characterisational level, since they indicate to us that the character concerned is precisely *the sort* of character who would eavesdrop. In the case of Maxim Maximych in *Bela* and Pechorin in *Taman* the eavesdropping is not so much psychologically as professionally motivated. It is the duty of an officer to be vigilant and suspicious in dangerous circumstances: in *Taman* it is Pechorin's duty, not the Cossack's; in *Bela* it is Maxim Maximych's, not the newly arrived Pechorin's (he does not know the local language); in *Princess Mary* the device is motivated by a general paranoia which Pechorin has helped to foster and which is partially justified by the plots which are being hatched against him. As Van Holk has pointed out Pechorin's 'inner activity' is manifested by 'sharpened watchfulness', being always 'on guard' (Van Holk, 1992: 549). Spying becomes second nature to him and may be attributed to the general atmosphere of *qui vive* which envelops him and all those serving in the Caucasus.[4]

Among current critical developments, the Caucasian dimension in Russian literature is at last attracting the attention that it deserves. Its crucial cultural significance is demonstrated in Susan Layton's recent study of the relationship between Russian literature and empire (Layton, 1994). Layton places *A Hero of Our Time* in the general context of the Russian fictionalisation of the Caucasus during the nineteenth century. Operating within a model broadly deriving from Edward Said, she sees the Caucasian literary context as figuratively articulating many of the suppressed and sublimated frustrations and insecurities of imperialist Russia: political, sociological and sexual. She also highlights the adaptive cultural challenge with which the Caucasus confronted the Russian incomer. Also significant in this regard is Kornblatt's study of the Cossacks in Russian literature (Kornblatt, 1992) which explores, among other things, the ethnic ambiguity of Cossackdom and the attraction of this for Russian writers. Both these works have influenced my approach to the setting of the novel in general and to the character of Maxim Maximych in the chapter which now follows.

Notes

1. E.g. Peace (1967).

2. Here and subsequently in this study the travelling narrator of *Bela* and *Maxim Maximych* is designated by an initial capital.

3. See Hyde (1992) for a full study of Nabokov's translation of the novel.

4. For a discussion of eavesdropping in the novel as a whole see Reid, 1977.

Bela

1. Telling the Tale

In a strictly narratological sense *Bela* is the most complex of the constituent stories of *A Hero of Our Time*. This is because, it is first told orally by a participative narrator, Maxim Maximych, to an anonymous writer of travel notes who then delivers it to the reader in written form. Traditionally critics have regarded this process as in general productive of the realistic effect which Lermontov, essentially a romantic, was striving to achieve in a socially relevant novel. This view is legitimate in that, at a first-time reading, it does appear that the voice of the traveller from Tiflis is not that of a writer of fiction at all, but, in modern terms a documentarist, aiming to record cultural realia and curiosities. Though it is certainly the case that the travel-note genre in itself was no guarantee of veracity, it was an already established, even passé genre by Lermontov's time with a hallowed association with the Caucasus in the form of Pushkin's *Journey to Arzrum* (1838). Less important than its veridical status, however, is its transcendent function as a mode of discourse: it is by definition metatextual since, as well as things essentially non-aesthetic, such as cultural mores and descriptive topography, it is also capable of representing and incorporating songs, narratives, stories, reminiscences, anything indeed which, whether actively sought out, or come upon by chance, imparts local colour.

It is not too far-fetched to apply some twentieth-century occupational metaphors to the travel-writer's role. There is something of the tourist in him and indeed since Pushkin's time Russians had regarded the Caucasus as, in effect, a tourist destination (*Princess Mary* representing these tendencies in their most sophisticated development). He has something of the aimlessness of the tourist snapping his initial impressions at random. But he is perhaps better regarded as a failed documentarist; he has lost his rolls of film which, he assures us, fishing for a compliment we cannot give, were not very good, and is having to start afresh. Gilroy (1989: 17) correctly observes that he is on the look-out for a story and it is precisely this which he associates with the travel-note genre: 'I was most eager to get some kind of yarn out of him – a desire common to all those who keep travel notes'(26).[1] This is not surprising: the other chief function of travel notes in this pre-photographic era was the evocation of exotic landscape and ethnic colour although the novel as a whole demonstrates the limitations of this function by enforcing a stylistic uniformity on landscape throughout, whether it is evoked by Pechorin or the Narrator.[2] In fact Lermontov, a romantic writer whose lyric verse and narrative poetry is dominated by Caucasian landscape, has moved, in *A Hero of Our Time*, towards a realist perspective on nature which relegates it to the functions of back-drop and pathetic fallacy. Only in *Taman* do we see traditional romantic atmosphere acquiring a dominant role, and that is ultimately revealed as a kind of aberration on the part of the hero.

The primacy of the search for 'story' on the part of the Narrator is best evidenced by the fact that, having acquired a superabundance of stories in *Maxim Maximych*, he abandons any further intention to 'contribute' to the collection: he has found what he has been looking for. The change in tone evident in the discourse of *Maxim Maximych* is also attributable to the same cause: he writes it after the acquisition of Pechorin's stories; he has no further need therefore to write in the travel-note mode ('...I won't burden you with descriptions of mountains, meaningless exclamations of rapture...which no-one would ever read' [62]).

If the Narrator is regarded as a 'story gatherer' it may be possible to define his functions in terms of the *skaz* collection which enjoyed popularity in Russia during the 1830s (Gogol's *Evenings on a Farm near Dikanka*; Pushkin's *Tales of Belkin*). However in these works the collector is a relatively shadowy figure and skaz is principally communicated through the style of the stories themselves. In *Bela* we have a dialogue between story-teller (Maxim) and collector which serves to sharply characterise both participants to the extent that the process of eliciting the story dialogically becomes equally as important as the story itself. The traditional view of the story, powerfully reinforced by Eikhenbaum, is that the 'device' of the travelling narrator is aimed largely at effecting a realistic portrayal of Pechorin. The logic is that since the travel-note mode is essentially realistic rather than fictional (we have for instance examples of early translators assuming that *A Hero of Our Time* was a true memoire of the Caucasus) the portrait of Pechorin which ultimately emerges will appear as a product or, more correctly, discovery of this realistic medium rather than simply a romantic fiction.

Eikhenbaum used the term 'motivation' to characterise the Narrator's insistence, throughout *Bela*, that the travel-note imperative should prevail over the fictional by ensuring that the Bela story is fed out to the reader only as and when it was originally imparted to him. The fiction is therefore that the Bela narrative is an adjunct or accompaniment to the predominant project of describing the Narrator's journey over the Krestovaya. This is facilitated by the fact that Maxim Maximych's story is skaz in the purest sense: he tells it to the Narrator in snatches and since he is *telling* he can be interrupted by the Narrator to elicit information which he as reader needs at a specific point (for instance his enquiries about the circumstances of Kazbich's abduction of Bela [57]) and even to supplement the limitations of Maxim's authorial omniscience regarding Pechorin's behaviour: 'Now you're a man who's lately been in the capital...Is it true that all the young people there are the same?' (54).

More important however than the mere fact of the oral medium of transmission is that the Narrator seeks to preserve the order and form of the transmission. We can legitimately infer a folkloristic or ethnographic motive in the punctilious determination to preserve exactly the manner and style of Maxim's telling as though it were a ballad or folk-narrative. Against this, paradoxically, we must place the fact that the Narrator is capable of dealing in a more arbitrary fashion with what might be considered more ethnically valuable, certainly more genuinely Caucasian material such as Kazbich's song to Azamat. This, originally in some kind of poetic form, is delivered in prose by Maxim Maximych (Bela's song, similarly delivered, remains in prose) and re-versed by the Narrator, who nevertheless feels it necessary to confess the fact to the reader in a note, thus satisfying the demands of documentary veracity. We know, of course, that the Narrator's definition of the role of the travel-note writer is itself fairly arbitrary. After Maxim has told him the first part of the Bela story he is sure that it is to...'describe and depict these magic scenes for others' (44) and he is urging us not to 'turn on a few pages' (46) to discover its denouement because we will miss a spectacular crossing of the Krestovaya. On the other hand by the beginning of *Maxim Maximych* he is convinced that his descriptions of mountains and 'meaningless exclamations of rapture' (62) would simply be a burden on the reader. The Narrator's insistence on preserving the Bela story in what is in essence its fabulaic form seems most obviously connected to the requirement to maximise the role both psychological, narrational and participative of Maxim Maximych. Indeed it is *Bela*, rather than its successor, which tells us most about Maxim. A central question about *Bela*, then, relates to the role of Maxim Maximych: what are we supposed to think about him? At this stage in the novel Pechorin is still a comparatively shadowy figure.

2. Maxim Maximych

However ironic in retrospect, the Narrator's conlusion, reached, we are asked to suppose, in Vladikavkaz *before* Pechorin's second meeting with Maxim Maximych, that Maxim 'is a sterling fellow' (61) (as though this were the purpose of telling the tale) is not so implausible. As already remarked Nicholas I had been satisfied with his reading of *A Hero of Our Time* as long as he thought that Maxim Maximych was going to occupy the central role (a somewhat short-lived satisfaction!).

It is precisely over the question of why Maxim Maximych is so important that there is least agreement among critics of *A Hero of Our Time*. Among western critics, where the influence of Eikhenbaum has been strong, we find a clear predilection for what may be termed structural rationalisation for

Maxim. Turner (1978: 8-9), for instance, sees a kind of chain of 'reliability' extending from the Narrator through Maxim and ultimately to Pechorin himself. Even the fact that Maxim's 'explanations of Pechorin's psychology' are 'severely curtailed' (9) by his provincial lack of understanding feeds into the structural ground plan of the novel, which is to delay the full internal characterisation of Pechorin until the Journal, so as not to prejudice the reader in advance. Peace (1967) also works on the same premiss, stressing the irony that when Maxim has fully performed his informative task he is cast aside in the story that bears his name.

More recent critics have been anxious to stress that Maxim's role is more complex, a view underpinned by Bakhtinian concern with dialogue and multi-voicing (see for instance Aizlewood, 1990 and Bagby, 1978). The longer studies by Gilroy (1989) and Barratt and Briggs (1989) have highlighted the complexity of the relationship between the Narrator and Maxim. Gilroy's general view is that the novel resists meaningful closure by producing paradox and irony. Thus Maxim's failure to understand Pechorin is seen as part of a general strategy to make the hero mysterious (Gilroy: 36) while *Bela* exemplifies a confusion of authorial voice, the Narrator trying to 'assert control' over what is happening, but being thwarted by circumstances (15). Barratt and Briggs are more concerned to stress the competing interests of the Narrator and Maxim. The Narrator is the social superior of Maxim and therefore looks down on him; on the other hand Maxim knows more about the Caucasus. The two men are involved in a struggle for supremacy but in Maxim's case the discrepancy between his social rank (with respect to the Narrator) and his status as Caucasian expert (and a European among 'inferior' Asiatics) means that he is a complex and contradictory character, sometimes humble and sometimes assertive (Barratt and Briggs: 17). What Barratt and Briggs' approach reveals is that a concentration on Maxim's character inevitably transcends the two principal narratorial levels of *Bela* – the travel notes and the Bela story – and demonstrates a fact about his structural role noted by Lotman (1977: 43), namely that 'the romantic antithesis between the Caucasian (the exotic) and the Russian (the commonplace) ethos is structurally cancelled out by an affirmation of the unity of the common man's (the naive) point of view [of Maxim Maximych]'. Barratt and Briggs are also concerned with the complexity of Maxim's role as narrator (Barratt and Briggs: 220). This lies in the fact that, while Maxim Maximych is narrating one of Pechorin's adventures, he is also narrating his own involvement in it. He plays off his role as onlooker against that of participant, and a superficial reading of the story reveals obvious areas of responsibility (telling Pechorin about Kazbich and Azamat's discussion about Karagyoz); however, as we shall see, there are perspectives from which Maxim would seem to be far more deeply implicated.

There is a solid and fairly influential tradition in Soviet scholarship which regards Maxim Maximych, partly because of his skaz role, as a character with strong affinities with the 'little man' who figured prominently in Russian literature of the 1830s (*The Bronze Horseman*; *The Tales of Belkin*; Gogol's tales). This dimension is developed by commentators such as Blagoi (1968: 39), Fokht (1975: 170), Usok (1976: 126) and Sokolov (1957: 227) who stress Maxim's naiveté and even childlike qualities which, on the principle, perhaps, of 'out of the mouths of babes and sucklings', are likely to enhance the realism of what he has to say. However it is a far cry from the little man of Pushkin and Gogol to an experienced frontier officer who has fought with Yermolov and commanded a fort in an only partially pacified area of the Russian empire. Most of Maxim's simplicity is relative to his sophisticated social superiors, the Narrator and Pechorin; the latter, as Layton (1994: 218) points out, is rendered more incomprehensible still by his Byronic affectation.

We do know that Lermontov was interested in Maxim's 'type' independently of its inclusion in *A Hero of Our Time*. His essay *The Caucasian* (1840-41) was intended as a character study for inclusion in a collection entitled *The Russians Taken From Real Life* which fell foul of the censor. The essay was only discovered in 1929. As one commentator has put it '*The Caucasian* is effectively an extended biography of Maxim Maximych which would have satisfied the legitimate interests of the readers of *A Hero of Our Time* about how such a personality developed' (Andronikov, 1965: 456). This rather vague statement leaves it open to us whether to interpret the shorter work as just useful background on Maxim's 'type' or as an explicatory addendum to an inherently open-ended work which had already acquired a defensive preface at its second edition.[3] There is no doubt however that much of *The Caucasian* is directly relevant to what we already know about Maxim Maximych or supplements or extends our knowledge about him.[4] Unlike *A Hero of Our Time* there is no narrating persona and the voice is more authoritative than that of the Narrator in *A Hero of Our Time*. It seems quite reasonable to suppose that it was precisely Lermontov's need to create the narrative persona of a tyro, an officer new to the Caucasus, in *A Hero of Our Time*, which prevented him biographising Maxim Maximych in the sort of objective manner we encounter in *The Caucasian*: the Narrator lacks the necessary information and experience and Maxim himself lacks both the objectivity and descriptive proficiency. *The Caucasian* suggests to us that, far from having a 'what you see is what you get' Maxim in *A Hero of Our Time*, we have an extremely restricted one, circumscribed by the structural demands of the novel. *The Caucasian* therefore explicates the implicit in Maxim's character.

The Caucasian, we are told, is a being half Russian, half Asiatic 'but a predilection for eastern customs *takes precedence* in him' [my italics][5] (137). If we are not aware of this when we meet him it is because he 'is ashamed of the fact in the presence of outsiders; that is arrivals from Russia' (137).

The Caucasian is also 'a remarkable man, deserving of every *respect and sympathy*' (137: my italics). He arrives in the Caucasus as a young man inspired by Pushkin's *Caucasian Captive* and hopes for heroic deeds. Life on the line proves dull and although he distinguishes himself for bravery he falls foul of boredom. As he ages he becomes 'gloomy and silent' (138). He is unmarried, though he once entertained the dream of living with a captive Circassian girl. As he gets older he values his friendship with a local chieftain and, under the latter's influence, he effectively goes native, dressing as a Circassian and, 'not knowing the history of Russia or European politics, has become attached to the poetic traditions of a martial people' (138). He takes 'his passion for all things Circassian to extraordinary lengths'; he has had many adventures with them which he will gladly retail (138). He prefers the Circassians to the Chechens and is impressed by their cleanliness. All these details amplify, albeit in some senses polemically, aspects of the character and opinions of Maxim Maximych in *A Hero of Our Time*. However *The Caucasian* concludes by extrapolating into the future. When past forty the Caucasian may return to Russia, getting himself invalided out of the army by the common method of exposing his leg to Circassian gunfire (one wonders about Grushnitsky in *Princess Mary* in this context); or he may get married and go to live in a fort, where his wife will preserve him from premature alcoholism. This, concludes Lermontov, is a portrait of a true Caucasian, though he lists several other semi-urbanised and inauthentic types.

The Caucasian is useful in suggesting a pragmatic explanation for the double narration of *Bela*. In *The Caucasian* Lermontov constructs his type as something alien both to himself and his reader. His *tipichnost'* in the Belinskian sense augments his predictability: Lermontov's narrative voice can confidently predict that if, reader, you meet him, he will act in such and such a way. His acculturation to the Asiatic way of life has gone almost far enough to allow him to be treated with the superior detachment of a nineteenth-century anthropologist. His life in the Caucasus has become a predictable cultural osmosis. Lermontov's narrative voice finds the process stunting because it is fraught with ethnic contradiction. As he reaches middle-age the Caucasian begins to draw ever closer to a native lifestyle and makes largely positive noises about the life of the tribesmen. This is too much for the narrative voice: when the Caucasian describes the Shapsugs, the ultimate die-hards in the fight for independence as 'clean', it retorts that only someone as prejudiced as a Caucasian could find anything clean in a Circassian hut. Clean in this, as in so many contexts, is shorthand for civilised approbation; the clean cannot be savage and, as we see from the Narrator's ethnological reactions in *Bela*, dirt and its analogues are the most reliable symptoms of savagery. Furthermore we learn that the Caucasian is likely to dissimulate when confronted by Russian travellers like the Narrator. But the reason for this dissimulation is not a mere intra-ethnic difference of class of the sort which, according to some commentators, makes Maxim Maximych uneasy with his social superiors. It arises from a desire to conceal the degree to which the Caucasian has become culturally assimilated. There is a fine line between being seen to have, in Layton's phrase, 'gone native in the Orient' (Layton, 1994: 216) and being seen to be a *bona fide* true son of Russia whose insight into the native tribes is attributable to observation and contact which falls well short of prejudicing one's national affiliation or ethnic preferences. It is the feral Caucasian in himself which Maxim seeks to conceal in his conversation with the Narrator. The Narrator in *Bela* is simultaneously the walking embodiment of the civilised and observant narrative voice of *The Caucasian* and of those 'arrivals from Russia' among whom both the narrating voice of *The Caucasian* and some of the readership may be numbered.

Maxim's reticence before the Narrator takes two forms. In the first place there is an unwillingness to praise the natives without some sort of reservation. At its extreme this implies a round condemnation of all of them: 'Fearful rogues these Asiatics are' (22).[6] This statement is made when the Narrator first meets Maxim Maximych with his bullock cart. Soon, however, Maxim reveals a more discriminating attitude. It is the Ossetian drivers who have elicited these remarks, members of the most degraded ethnic group in the Caucasus[7] whose pacified state is underlined by their work as bearers for the Russians under their association with the pacific ox, rather than, in the case of the Circassians and Chechens, the warhorse. Durylin calls this generalisation of Maxim Maximych's a 'group judgment' (1940: 42) on behalf of the imperialist establishment but the situation is clearly more complex than this, the utterance, and others of similar content, being encoded with a view to the immediate context of the baggage train and the status of the hearer as an arrival from Russia. Besides this we also find Maxim making some exceptions to his original point of view in regard to other ethnic groups: 'Say what you like about our friends the Kabardinians or the Chechens – *robbers and vagabonds* they may be, but they're plucky devils for all that. Why, this lot don't even bother about weapons' (25) [my italics]. As soon as the element of inter-ethnic comparison is introduced we have some confusion too about the ethnic intentionality of Maxim's statement. *Prima facie* he is making a general comparison between *ethoi* as opposed to *ethnoi* such as a soldier of any nationality might reasonably be expected to make. On the other hand it is unlikely that the warlike, arms-bearing Chechens and Kabardinians would hold any other view of the Ossetians themselves than that articulated by the Caucasian, Maxim, from the depths of his knowledge and respect for them. Indeed, after he has made what is in effect a favourable assessment of the Chechens concealed under a general dismissal of Asiatics in general, symbolised by the Ossetians, the Narrator asks him almost suspiciously: 'How long have you spent in Chechnya?' (25). Durylin points out the frequency with which Maxim Maximych uses terms for robbers and thieves to characterise the Chechens (Durylin, 1940: 47). It is used not only collectively but of Kazbich, Kazbich's horse (a robber's horse) and of Bela when she sees Kazbich on her father's horse and her 'brigand's' blood comes out in her. Clearly this designation comes from the perspective of an upholder of law and order: tribesmen in occu- pied territories who were still waging war against the Russians were defined simply as offenders against law, rather than as members of a guerrilla army.

The other important way in which the Narrator's presence constrains Maxim is that, as a newcomer to the region, he requires the cultural realia in the Bela story to be explained in terms which are intellectually accessible. Lotman (1977: 43-4) treats this issue in the context of cultural codes and it is particularly in evidence in Maxim's description of the wedding ceremony at which Pechorin first sees Bela. A wedding is a predictable focus of ethnic specificity and one cannot safely assume that the nuptial ceremonial of one culture will be replicated in the next. 'What happens at their wedding celebra- tions?' is the Narrator's inevitable question (28). Maxim's reply translates the ceremony into terms familiar to the Narrator: 'Oh, nothing special...when it gets dark they have what we'd call a ball in the best room with some poor old fellow strumming away on a three stringed...I can't remember the name, anyway it's like a balalaika...the host's youngest daughter sang him a... – what shall I say? – a sort of compliment' (29). The effect of such a description is to down-play the exotic, and, superficially, it might be taken for that form of perception familiar to anthropologists whereby the alien culture is read in terms of the perceiving culture, its otherness being overcome by a translation into the familiar. However, apart from this cultural translation, there are also elements in Maxim's description which exploit the familiar equation between savagery and defilement: '...some filthy tramp on a miserable broken down hack...' (29). Certainly these aspects of the picture are not suggestive of a great and warlike people but of a degraded one. If Maxim admires the natives he is concealing it here, in contrast to his enthusiastic depictions of the heroine Bela and Kazbich's horse Karagyoz. Again however all of the latter would be acceptable objects of admiration for a red-blooded soldier, whatever his ethnic origins.

Read against *The Caucasian,* Maxim becomes a more complex character because of his ethnic ambiguity and moreover through his evident efforts to conceal the latter. The degree of acculturation implied brings him close to that other ethnic group of the Caucasus – the Cossacks – which are a presence in *A Hero of Our Time* but provide no major characters. The Cossacks represent a group form of acculturation through their intermarriage with local populations and their long collective presence in the Caucasus. Their *stanitsas* were an important element too in the gradual imperial encroachment on the lands of the native tribes. Yet Maxim is not a Cossack. Unmarried and relatively socially isolated, he cannot aspire or contribute to any pioneering presence in the Caucasus. Simply in the space of a lifetime, Caucasians like Maxim, in the tradition of Marlinsky, could pass through assimilation to the native life-style as far as any individual could while still remaining loyal to the imperial power. Much of what is said here about Maxim, applies in differing degree to Pechorin too. Isolation is qualitative rather than quantitative. It does not depend solely on the length of time spent in the Caucasus. Van der Eng (1993: 32-3) points out that, for all his long sojourn in the Caucasus, Maxim cannot be taken for a Circassian, whereas we know (from *Princess Mary*) that Pechorin can. *Princess Mary* also confirms that identification with a culture other than one's own is fraught with ambiguities which go to the heart of the imperial condition: the fashionable ladies of Piatigorsk are as much under threat from the rampages of Byronic Circassian look-alikes, as from the occasional incursions of genuine Circassian abreks.

3.   Inter-ethnic Relations

The interaction between the natives and the colonials in *Bela* is not simply problematised in the telling. The relationship between those commanding the fort and the natives outside is profoundly ambiguous. It is complicated by the fact that on both sides there are distinct interest groups.[8] The ostensible polarities between Russian occupier and the Chechen population on the one hand and between loyal (*mirnye*) and insurgent tribesmen on the other were in practice more confused. Thus newly pacified regions would nevertheless contain or be visited by insurgents: even the family of the loyal prince in *Bela* contains a son, Azamat, who is ready to leave and join the rebels. Kazbich is clearly an *abrek* (outlaw) who, as Maxim recognises, is only making a pretence of loyalty. Durylin (1940: 56-8) notes that the *kunachestvo* between Maxim and both Kazbich and the prince, Bela's father, was probably undertaken officially by Maxim as a way of keeping tabs on prominent people in his neighbour-hood. Kunachestvo obliged its participants to protect their fellow *kunak* while under their roof and to avenge any insult to him. Durylin describes it as an insurance policy in a Caucasus dominated by blood feuds but, in the obligations of vendetta which it imposed, it must clearly have contributed to a general situation of endemic violence.

Several things emerge from Maxim's *kunachestvo*: 1) he would have been obliged to help Kazbich when the latter was attacked by Azamat and, as Maxim feared, by the latter's family; 2) he is obliged to avenge the mis-fortunes which befall Bela's father: the abduction of Bela; his death; the theft of his horse; the death of Bela herself; 3) he would have been obliged to avenge the theft of Kazbich's horse, particularly since this takes place on his own territory. Regarded in this way, of course, the situation is quite irredeemable in terms of the native code of honour, not least because each of Maxim's kunaks has seriously wronged the other: the prince has wronged Kazbich because his son has taken the latter's horse; Kazbich has wronged the prince by killing him and taking his horse. Maxim confesses himself nonplussed as to why Azamat's father has been killed by Kazbich, whereas in fact the latter is carrying out the vendetta which Maxim himself should have carried out on his behalf. Kazbich's role here, as zealot enforcing the revenge ethic which others have reneged on, recalls the progress of Hadzhi Abrek's vendetta against Bey Bulat in Lermontov's *Hadzhi Abrek*: Bey Bulat has abducted a young woman, Leila, and her father asks Hadzhi Abrek to recover her. Hadzhi Abrek, however, enacts his pre-existing vendetta against Bey Bulat by killing Leila whom Bey Bulat loves and bringing her head back to her father. The latter is punished for having failed to avenge her himself. Kazbich's ultimate vengeance is the murder of Bela as satisfaction for the theft of his horse, again, an act which should have been rectified by Maxim. Maxim, who by this time has moved into a *locus parentis* is thus left in a similar situation to the father in *Hadzhi Abrek*.

The second part of the Bela story, narrated after the crossing of the Krestovaya, is dominated by Maxim's role as surrogate father. This perhaps may be seen as a mild exercise of his duty as kunak to her father, but it is ineffective, since he fails to protect her and is compromised in another sense because it grows out of his sublimated desire to have had a native girl like Bela for himself. Viewed all in all, Maxim's dereliction of moral duty in the story is considerable, certainly for one so versed in Caucasian ways as he appears to be. It is easy to say that the contradictions in the vendetta system make it inevitable that such situations will come about; it may also be claimed with some justification that, if Maxim is carrying out what is in effect intelligence work via the native institution of *kunachestvo*, and cementing contacts with loyal (the prince) and disloyal (Kazbich) alike, then a subversion of loyalty in the strict sense could be the only outcome of such cynical exploitation.[9] There is indeed some flavour of colonial exploitation in the story: beer drinking (Durylin,1940: 59), like whisky drinking among the American Indians, was generally a sign of pernicious Russian influence and a departure from Muslim prohibition.[10] Azamat typifies the native corrupted by contact with civilisation. However it is Pechorin who engineers this corruption and, since he is elsewhere in the novel the figure who consistently precipitates violent action, it is perhaps now time to assess his contribution to the ethical mayhem in which Maxim becomes embroiled.

4.   Pechorin and Kazbich

There seems little doubt that the tissue of counter-obligations revealed in the story would not have emerged without Pechorin's intervention. Indeed what is remarkable is the ingenuity with which he subverts the native moral checks and balances by both imitating and estranging a given moral situation. What Maxim overhears when he ventures out of the wedding reception for some fresh air is essentially the fabula of the final Bela plot, but *in negativo*. This is moreover an intra-ethnic plot which emerges, as it were, from the folk, independently of Russian participation, so that, without being fortuitously lighted on by a curious Russian, it would never have been discovered, nor, more importantly, have taken place.

The two interlocutors who are the two ethnic protagonists in the story have different interests which to some extent represent their different social standing. Azamat, the spoilt son of a chief on good terms with the Russians, nevertheless aspires to become an abrek and fight against them. For this he requires a horse and is willing to barter his sister for it. This weakness of Azamat's, first mentioned by Maxim in the context of his stealing a goat for ten roubles, suggests a person compromised by his close relationship with the Russians. Kazbich, on the other hand, is characterised in flattering terms by Maxim Maximych, refuses to haggle over cattle he brings to the fort and is a genuine abrek, the fact that he can play the system with respect to soldiers like Maxim, notwithstanding. To this extent Kazbich is a fulfilled individual, one of a very small number in the novel (perhaps Yanko in *Taman* is the only other) and as such, wanting nothing and strong-willed, is immovable in the face of Azamat's blandishments, and this despite the fact that he too is attracted to Bela. He will simply not trade his horse with which his status and success as a partisan is so closely associated, for a prince's daughter. For this reason therefore the conversation overheard by Maxim Maximych is bound to be unproductive in its outcome. Kazbich is not planning any move against Azamat's father or family and Azamat is not going to gain anything by stealing Bela for him. Kazbich is proof against intrigue because he adheres to the local code of honour in its prophylactic rather than reactive form. His coat of mail even forestalls Azamat's puny attack on him so that this too, along with the whole course of their conversation, seems to have been foreseen by him.

Such is the cultural sketch which Maxim presents to Pechorin perhaps as an instructive example of the comparative demeanour of the two natives. Little does he know that he has imparted this archeplot to a man who once wrote that 'the idea of evil cannot enter a man's mind without his wanting to fulfill it in practice' (127). Without this information would Pechorin ever have dared to go ahead with the abduction of Bela? His behaviour in the rest of the novel would suggest not. His ideal is for others to be so manipulated and misled that they freely present him with what he wishes to achieve. Without this precious information he might still have persuaded Azamat to steal his sister on an *a fortiori* principle: after all, he has already stolen for Pechorin the best goat from his father's flock. Yet it is difficult to imagine what incentive there would be for Azamat to do such a thing; what is vital in Maxim's revelation is the extent of Azamat's longing for Kazbich's horse. And not only this: there is the thwarting of this concupiscence by Kazbich's refusal. This refusal, however, becomes Pechorin's assent. Pechorin has edged Kazbich's refusal aside; double-like supplanting him, he says yes where

Kazbich says no. Alone with Azamat in the night, Kazbich has insisted that he will not steal Bela and that Azamat shall not have his horse, and yet, a short time after, it turns out that Azamat does steal Bela and does take Kazbich's horse. The difference between Pechorin and Kazbich is that the first was willing to say yes where the second said no. The role of Azamat however is the same in either case: he is a thief and is willing to steal to effect the exchange. By refusing to exchange Karagyoz Kazbich effectively stops Azamat from stealing. In appropriating the plot of the horse/woman exchange, Pechorin is in a position diametrically opposed to Kazbich: he wants the woman and does not want the horse. In this important way Pechorin, however much he may, to use Layton's phrase, have released 'the "Asia" within him' is in axiological terms diametrically opposed to the native code (Layton, 1994: 17). Pechorin also starts from a position of having nothing to barter with. However he is able to sing the praises of Karagyoz more effectively even than Kazbich precisely because he does not own him and has everything to gain by having him stolen.

Early commentators saw in this and similar Machiavellian tactics on Pechorin's part a demonic quality. Gaining information about individual weaknesses by quasi-superhuman means, fortuitous eavesdroppings in particular, Pechorin proceeds to undo the firmest intentions towards good and, in this case, rearranges the elements of a moral situation so as to create its polar opposite. However there are more pragmatic ways of reading the situation. Challenged by Maxim after the abduction of Bela Pechorin argues (in effect) that, since, among the Circassians, abduction is a recognised way of acquiring a wife, Bela will now be considered married by the natives and that, besides, 'an uncivilised Circassian girl should be glad to have a nice husband like him' and also that Kazbich 'was a brigand and deserved to be punished' (p.36). Both of these explanations are Eurocentric rationalisations. As principles for action they do not stand up to universalisation: not all Circassian insurgents should have their horses stolen as a matter of principle or all Circassian maidens be married to Russian officers for their own good. Although Pechorin is clearly attracted by the 'plot' potential of the relationship between Azamat and Kazbich, he can only exploit it by reason of the profoundly ambiguous moral standards which the Russian occupation has introduced into the Caucasus. On the one hand Maxim Maximych is willing to cultivate bonds with those like Kazbich whom he considers to be brigands; on the other privileged local families like Bela's are softened up and their children corrupted by contact with the Russian soldiery. Russian conduct, then, is depicted as, at best amoral (in the case of Maxim who adopts aspects of the Circassian code without responsibility) if not downright immoral (in the case of Pechorin's attempts to out-brigand the brigands).

It is an irony of the novel's structure that, on a first reading, all the psychological and cultural information which would enable us to make sense of Pechorin's escapade with the natives lies ahead of us. Deprived of this we are left to interpret it as an exotic adventure, remarkable enough to impress a veteran like Maxim Maximych but probably par for the course in a romantic environment of hill forts and wild tribesmen. What the whole novel unfolds, however, is the deeply symptomatic nature of Pechorin's behaviour for the officer class of the Russian army: among whom are numbered Grushnitskys, Vuliches and Pechorins as well as Caucasians like Maxim Maximych. Above all *Bela* sets the limits to 'going native' in the Caucasus. The Caucasian look-alike, Pechorin, who scares Princess Mary later in the novel in his Circassian garb, seems a stranger among the people he emulates. He has more in common with Azamat whom he has corrupted than with Kazbich whom he is instrumental in dispossessing. Kazbich, by contrast, remains uncompromised to the end. He is able to come in on the deal between Pechorin and Azamat which dispossesses him. In acting as the sole avenger in the story and therefore sole custodian of this dimension of the native ethos he recovers the archeplot which Pechorin has stolen from him with Maxim's help. By killing Azamat's father and taking his horse he avenges Azamat's theft and at the same time makes a kind of equine restitution. He also eliminates the pacified chieftain whose co-operation with the Russians was a component cause of the ills which befell him. Mounted on this horse he is able to taunt Bela on the battlements showing how the plot which secured her abduction at the price of his horse has now taken the life of her father and provided a new horse. Maxim is taunted too for allowing these things to have taken place unavenged.

In the curious episode which follows Maxim orders his sentry to shoot Kazbich, we must assume to avenge the death of Bela's father. It is significant that he will not shoot at his kunak himself. When the sentry protests that Kazbich 'don't keep still' (51) Maxim replies 'you tell him to' (51) and laughs. Perhaps he knows what will happen next: as soon as Kazbich sees the flash of powder, light travelling faster than sound and sound than bullets, he jumps aside and escapes unharmed. It is hard to imagine that Maxim, who reveals himself to be an expert in such matters at the end of *The Fatalist*, would not be aware of this ballistic phenomenon. Perhaps he has satisfied honour by shooting at Kazbich and missing; as Barratt and Briggs suggest he also seems to believe that the blade is more certain than the bullet, which will certainly be so in the unfortunate case of Bela (Barratt and Briggs, 1989: 111). Nevertheless this incident with the gun places Kazbich firmly among the major male characters of the novel – Pechorin, Maxim Maximych, Grushnitsky, Vulich – figures crucially involved with firearms. This incident stands in its implications midway between the murderous duel of *Princess Mary* and the suicide of *The Fatalist*. In *The Fatalist* the reasons for the misfire remain mysterious and unseen within the mechanism of the gun; in the case of Kazbich, as we have seen, the laws of physics offer a likely explanation for his survival; in *Princess Mary*, however, the vagaries of ballistics have been entirely supplanted in determining the outcome by cunning on Grushnitsky's part and counter-cunning on Pechorin's in discovering and profiting from the former's plot to disarm him.

Kazbich's abduction of Bela wrapped in a yashmak exactly parallels her first abduction by Azamat. His killing of her ensures a loss as permanent for Pechorin and Maxim as his own of Karagyoz. However Bela's lingering death allows us to see which of these two has been punished the most. Considered without reference to its structural function the death scene does seem to be unnecessarily prolonged. One critic supposes that this is done for the sadistic gratification of the male readership (Andrew, 1988: 65).[11] However its structural purpose is clearly to differentiate sharply between the reactions of Maxim and Pechorin to a single tragic situation so as to achieve the maximum contrast (in Maxim's favour) between these two characters prior to the catastrophe of *Maxim Maximych*.

Kazbich is not taken or killed by Pechorin and Maxim because, although his horse has been shot from under him by Pechorin, he is only wounded in the shoulder by Maxim, who had 'fired my shot without taking aim' (having previously told Pechorin 'don't fire...save your shot. We'll catch him anyway') (56). Despite this, Maxim, having fired, finds himself out of shot and thus unable to pick Kazbich off as he makes his escape on foot. This, plus the postscript about Kazbich in a red beshmet fighting with the Shapsugs (the most war-like of the mountain tribes) and dodging the bullets, raises him to an almost mythical status as the one true Caucasian in the novel, as Andrew puts it 'a man alone in the world of nature to an extent to which Pechorin can only aspire.' (Andrew, 1988: 63). Yet, predictably, Maxim remains sceptical about him, musing that this could hardly be the same Kazbich. The nature of Maxim's attitude to Kazbich is more problematical and puzzling than his attitude to Pechorin which is one of naive incomprehension. Do Maxim's multiple failures to kill Kazbich reflect incompetence, Hamletic uncertainty or a subversive refusal to kill a man who 'brigand though he was' was still a kunak (36)? This uncertainty extends as well to his tolerance of Pechorin's behaviour and his failure to adequately discipline him. Perhaps all of these things have less importance within the totality of the novel since Maxim has also been constructed, for all his depth, as a disposable character. In organic terms, in the context of his role in the novel as a whole, his function is perfectly articulated. As a character in his own right he remains as much a fragment as the *Caucasian* essay which was meant to elucidate him, an enigma who momentarily appears to be an adequate fictional end in his own right, but, like the Circassians in *Bela* and the water-takers of Piatigorsk, is exploited in the interests of a more sophisticated plot.

Notes

1. Translations and page references are from the Penguin translation unless otherwise stated: Mikhail Lermontov, *A Hero of Our Time*, translated and intoduced by Paul Foote, Penguin, Harmondsworth, 1966.

2. See introduction, note 2.

3. The desire to see *A Hero of Our Time* as a finished work has gone hand in hand with its rise in canonical status. The plea of recent critics for a recognition of the work's open-endedness may be little more that a recognition of fact. Much depends on whether we believe that the narrator's claim to possess another publishable notebook of Pechorin's is merely a rhetorical device or an intimation by Lermontov that more was to follow.

4. Of non-Russian critics Gifford (1950: 104) was the first to recognise the significance of *The Caucasian* in relation to Maxim Maximych.

5. This and subsequent quotations from *The Caucasian* are translated by me from Kavkazets, in M.Yu. Lermontov, *Sobranie sochinenia v chetyrekh tomakh*, E. Zhezlova et al., Moscow, khudozhestvennaia literatura, 1965, pp.137-140.

6. Compare *The Caucasian*: 'a good people only they're such Asiatics' (138).

7. On this see Durylin (1940: 42-3).

8. There is some disagreement regarding the ethnicity of the tribe from which Bela comes. This, however, seems to have been brought about by a confusion in the use of the terms Tatar and Circassian which, however, was not Lermontov's alone, but simply reflected local Russian usage of the day. Durylin suggests that 'Circassian' was the general term for the tribes of the Caucasus, Tatar being used of their language and also to stress their Muslim affiliation (Durylin, 1940, 49). Austin (1986: 162) speculates that women were known as 'Circassians' and men as 'Tatars' but the usage in the novel does not bear this out. There is general agreement, however, that the fort in *Bela* was in Chechnya and that Bela and her family were Chechens, Austin (1986: 161) suggests that the Caucasian language which Lermontov was known to have been learning was Azebaijani which served as a lingua franca in the Caucasus but he does not confirm the identity of the native words used in *Bela*. 'Bela' itself is Turkic, meaning, appropriately enough, 'sad' in addition to its obvious Indo-european resonances. Aizelwood considers the multi-lingual nature of the Caucasus to be an important feature of the novel and links this to multiple voicing generally in the work (1990: 42) and while these aspects can be exaggerated, it is significant that the novel contains instances of Russian, French, Italian, Turkic and Little Russian or Ukrainian.

9. On the ambiguities of Maxim's position in this context see Scotto (1992: 250-1).

10. Maxim Maximych himself, however, does not drink.

11. The question of the gender of the readership is however not necessarily to be inferred from the address to the 'dear sirs' in the introduction to the second edition. Layton is ambivalent about the role of a female readership for Caucasian literature, assuming however that women readers would have delighted in the macho derring-do of Marlinsky's heroes and that men would have been uneasy about them reading such material (Layton, 1994: 153 and 155). On the other hand there is certainly some evidence to suggest that women were among the most avid readership just after the novel's publication. S.A. Burach, for instance, writing a negative review of the novel in 1845 cites three typically approving female salon reactions to the novel and one negative male reaction with which he is reluctantly forced to agree. (See Zhuravleva, 1991: 3-11.)

Maxim Maximych

1. Autotelic and Heterotelic Tensions

Maxim Maximych is clearly the most functionally oriented story in *A Hero of Our Time* since one of its roles is to furnish the narrator with Pechorin's notebooks which will supply the rest of the novel. It is true also that of all the stories it is the one least able to stand on its own, not only for the reason just stated, but because reader orientation in it depends so much upon information gleaned about all three major actants from what has already been unfolded in *Bela*.

Turner uses the term 'autotelic' (having an intrinsic aim or purpose) to characterise stories which are able to stand independent of a collection (Turner, 1978: 15) and it seems to be practical to define the opposite characteristic (the inability of a story to exist independently – not in itself a negative feature but simply a consequence of the organic status of that story) as 'heterotelic'. *Maxim Maximych* therefore has to be accounted for in terms of imperatives which lie outside it; however this is not to say that it does not have a *structural* integrity as a story in its own right. Indeed it exhibits almost classical structural form, observing strict unity of time, place and theme and in formal terms moving from a clearly defined prologue and complication through a crisis to denouement and epilogue. What is produced in this process is both new to the reader and complete in itself: the spurning of Maxim by Pechorin is a discrete and discontinuous event with the same kind of autonomous status in the novel as Pechorin's experiences in *Taman* or the death of Vulich in *The Fatalist*. It is the case therefore that there are important autotelic features in the story, the fate of Maxim being the most prominent.

A first-time reader encountering *Maxim Maximych* in isolation (without the contextual benefit of the rest of the novel) would be able to appreciate the core thrust of the story despite being deprived of the background on the characters available to someone who had read *Bela* first. Such a reader would grasp that Pechorin has been a figure of some considerable interest and importance for both of the other characters in the story and would suppose that Maxim's hope that Pechorin would come out to meet him was not illusory since it appears also to be shared by a narrator who himself is interested to meet this figure. The degree of suspense created by Maxim Maximych's vigil would be sufficient in itself to establish for such a reader the profundity of Maxim's attachment to the unknown Pechorin. Then by a dialectical anti-thesis the same reader would be affected by the cool reception received by Maxim and by Pechorin's abrupt departure despite Maxim's insistence that he should stay. The epilogue would be no less clear to such an 'uninformed' reader as to one who was *Bela*-aware: neither reader has suspected that the departed Pechorin kept a journal; both however can understand why Maxim must want to be rid of it at this time. The reason why so much of what is essential to the story lies in the autotelic rather than the heterotelic is to be found partly in the intensity of Maxim's emotion which is initially conveyed by his delight at hearing of Pechorin's arrival and confirmed by his unneces-sary vigil at the gates. The story creates a drama of expectation and a tragedy of disappointment which function independently of any previous set of circumstances of which the reader may be ignorant.

However it is also the case that the intensity of emotion so carefully nurtured in the Maxim of the story has a vital heterotelic function. Characters in fiction are frequently hierarchised by critics in terms of sympathy and antipathy, minor characters commonly evoking few of these emotions in the reader and major characters and protagonists being so established and described as to evoke many more. As in life so in literature, the characters we care most about or feel most about (even negatively) become the most important figures in their context. It is therefore important for the establishment of Pechorin as the main character in the novel as a whole that other figures be shown to feel strongly about him, and this is indeed what happens as the reader proceeds. In *Princess Mary* the principal female characters feel extremes of love and hate towards Pechorin which they will carry with them for life and Maxim too displays an extraordinary degree of devotion to Pechorin which, when definitively cast aside by the latter, turns into permanent disillusionment. *Maxim Maximych* is the turning point in the life of its eponymous hero. He will never be the same again:

> Good kindly Maxim Maximych was now the pig-headed, crotchety captain. And the reason? All because Pechorin had without thinking, or for some other reason, offered his hand when Maxim Maximych had wanted to embrace him. It is sad to see a young man's fondest hopes and dreams shattered when the rose coloured veil is plucked away and he sees the actions and feelings of men for what they are. But he still has the hope of replacing his old illusion with others, just as fleeting, but also just as sweet. But what can replace them in a man of Maxim Maximych's age? Inevitably, he becomes crusty and withdrawn (73).

Maxim's extreme devotion is thus a powerful sympathetic device in the overall strategy for characterising Pechorin and the full implication of this emotion can only be brought out by the tragic denouement of the story. Paradoxically it is only in the emotional destruction of Maxim Maximych that the full depth of his devotion to Pechorin can be properly seen.

The attachment psychology which underlies the characterisation of Pechorin in the novel as a whole likewise requires this sacrificing of the attached character (Bela, Vera etc.) and this because of the dynamic of sympathetic characterisation and in particular of its inherent transcendence. The character whose sympathy is used to establish the status of the major character must first be made to seem significant and sympathetic to the reader in his or her own right. Indeed, a direct proportion operates: the more sympathic the figure to the reader the more that figure's sympathy or attachment to other fictional characters will be taken seriously. Thus the generator of sympathy for the protagonist is effective inasmuch as he or she appropriates sympathy for his or her self. The elimination of this generator of sympathy becomes necessary so that the latter should not turn into a competitor with the protagonist for the reader's sympathy. This process has been long recognised in fiction as the principle of the dispensibility of characters: a character who is no longer needed in a narrative is disposed of. In the case of Maxim Maximych this convention has become particularly obtrusive, the device laid bare. At the *Bela* stage of the novel the reader has no need to suppose that Maxim Maximych is not going to continue in the role of the principal character which he seems to occupy at that stage. Moreover the narrator goes out of his way to suggest that the main purpose in his characterisation of Maxim Maximych has been to elicit our sympathy for him: 'Don't you agree, though, that Maxim Maximych is a sterling fellow? If you do, then I shall be amply rewarded for my – perhaps too lengthy – tale' (61). This fattening up of Maxim represents one half of the process whereby his sympathy for Pechorin is established, i.e. his sympathy has to be seen to be worth having. At the end of *Bela* we have no reliable means of measuring the degree of his devotion to Pechorin. Indeed the conclusion of *Bela* has shown Maxim lavishing his devotion on a Circassian girl while Pechorin looks coldly on. However one of the functions of the prolonged death of Bela is to demonstrate Maxim's capacity for devotion (as it indeed demonstrates Pechorin's incapacity). In *Maxim Maximych* Maxim demonstrates the application of that capacity to Pechorin. The dynamics of attachment run as follows: 1) the narrator becomes attached to Maxim; 2) Maxim becomes attached to Bela; 3) Maxim shows the depth of his attachment at her deathbed; 4) the reader, it is hoped, is by now attached to Maxim; 5) Maxim demonstrates his attachment to Pechorin by his delight on hearing of his arrival in Vladikavkaz; 6) Maxim shows the depth of his attachment in his prolonged wait for Pechorin; 7) Maxim is spurned by Pechorin; 8) Maxim becomes disillusioned.

There are several features of importance here. A perusal of the stages of what is a complex emotional process will reveal certain emotional affinities between Maxim's two major attachments: to Pechorin and to Bela. In both cases devotion is demonstrated by a vigil: the wait for Bela to die; the wait for Pechorin to appear. Devotion is measured by a willingness to wait: the longer one waits, the more devoted one is. Secondly the sequel to waiting is in each case the loss of the object of devotion: the death of Bela in the first case; the indifference of Pechorin in the second. Thirdly the degree of devotion to the object is measurable by the reaction of the subject to its loss: Maxim's grief at the death of Bela and at his final parting with Pechorin. Devotion therefore makes itself known in a wishing for the presence of the object of devotion and a grieving for its loss. On the latter point the Bela incident serves as an important precedent for what happens in *Maxim Maximych*, for, though grieved by Bela's death, Maxim is able to continue his life much as before, whereas the 'loss' of Pechorin promises to have a permanent and profoundly deleterious effect on the rest of his life.

This closing up of Maxim Maximych, intimating that he will henceforth give up on life, and that the best is now behind him, allows us as readers to review what we know of his biography from a perspective of closure. We can now confidently say that he has had two loves in his life – Bela and Pechorin – and has lost them both. Barbara Heldt points out that both *Maxim Maximych* and *The Fatalist* are essentially male/male stories in terms of the gender relations between the protagonists and that a function of these male/male stories is to act as resolutions or rationalisations to the male/female stories which are juxtaposed to them in the novel (Heldt, 1987: 30). There are several reasons for disagreeing with this as a general view of the novel's structure (it is not clear to all critics, for instance, that *The Fatalist* does offer any kind of 'resolution') but it does serve to highlight the fact that *Maxim Maximych* enacts on a homosexual level, or homosocial, at least, what has been enacted in *Bela* on the heterosexual level.

In both cases Pechorin spurns the advances of one devoted to him. The question of the homo-erotic dimension to Maxim's devotion to Pechorin cannot be ruled out and indeed the importance of both homo-erotic and narcissistic motifs in the novel generally has recently been explored by A. Hansen Löve (Hansen Löve, 1993). The latter points out particularly the narcissistic social role of the dandy and also the strong feminine traits in the description of Pechorin in *Maxim Maximych*, something noted by other critics too, but without much concentration on the possible psycho-sexual implications. Certainly the introduction of this imagery by the narrator does allow us to state, at least metaphorically, that in *Maxim Maximych* Maxim spends many hours eagerly awaiting a *femme de trente ans* who then jilts him and breaks his heart. However it is difficult to take this line of interpretation much further, the more so since such a theme could not be developed in any significant way given prevailing attitudes in nineteenth-century Russia, even if Lermontov had wished to do so.

Two more conventional explanations for Maxim's attitude to Pechorin in *Maxim Maximych* do present themselves, however. The first of these is provided, in effect, by the Narrator at the beginning of the story: 'We greeted each other like old friends...what a strange fellow he is' (62-3). Clearly the narrator and Maxim are not long-lost friends: the story thus early establishes an unorthodox view of friendship which echoes that already encountered in the Bela story: 'You'll find it a bit dull here, so don't let's stand on ceremony. Just call me Maxim Maximych, if you don't mind' (27). Compare with this Maxim's re-encounter with the narrator in *Maxim Maximych*: 'I gave him the use of my room. He did not stand on ceremony and even went so far as to slap me on the back...' (62-3). A picture emerges of a frontier region in which the usual rules of formality and social differentiation are relaxed or suspended; similarly the distinction between friend, acquaintance and stranger becomes flexible and blurred. From an anthropological point of view this is a similar process in the intra-Russian context to what was discussed in the foregoing chapter concerning the erosion of the native *kunachestvo* through Russian interaction. Maxim's characterisation of Pechorin in this context shows an extreme interchangeability of lexis from 'bosom friend' (*drug kadychnyi*) to *priatel'* to direct modes of address such as *drazhaishii*, 'dearest friend'. If we add to this the incapacity for friendship revealed by Pechorin elsewhere in the novel we have a doubly tragic misreading of the situation by Maxim: a Caucasian's too-ready willingness to predicate the term 'friend' to a subject incapable of friendship on any definition.

In an autotelic reading of the story the reader, without the hindsight of *Bela*, might interpret the unresponsiveness of the unknown Pechorin to the natural mutability of human affection over time: this would be the most likely contextualisation under such circumstances. However we can seek for other reasons, if not within the context of the novel as a whole then in the light of what we have learnt from *Bela*. Why does Maxim Maximych mention Bela's name to Pechorin? In one sense the reader requires it to be done so that, just as a visible and tangible Pechorin has made his appearance at last in the novel, a visible and tangible connection can be made between this Pechorin and the Pechorin of *Bela*. It is best described as a tactless allusion on Maxim's part. But it is also a strange one. We can indeed imagine the roles reversed with Pechorin not wishing to bring the matter up, knowing how it had both compromised and upset Maxim Maximych. And yet it is possible to read Maxim's allusion to Bela as a kind of desperate appeal to Pechorin to take notice of him and give him the time he feels he deserves: to have been through 'Bela' together is reason for them to talk. Pechorin, however, thinks it reason not to. We do not really find out what Pechorin feels about Maxim Maximych, although we may appear to do so. It is usually assumed that Pechorin's *treatment* of Maxim in the story represents what he thinks of the latter but this cannot truly be the case. Pechorin 'has no time' for Maxim in a literal rather than a metaphorical sense. In fact his behaviour in *Maxim Maximych* is one of avoidance of Maxim Maximych rather than of any determination to insult him (we will learn later that Pechorin is particularly ingenious when he *does* wish to insult). In fact the meeting with Maxim is an unfortunate hitch in what otherwise would have been a perfect getaway on Pechorin's part: he has lain low at the colonel's house since hearing of Maxim's arrival. When they finally do meet the only emotion which Pechorin shows is when Maxim mentions Bela. It is therefore reasonable to assume that Pechorin is avoiding Maxim because of the Bela incident.

The first-time reader, who has only the benefit of *Bela* behind him, can only speculate upon the reasons for Pechorin's reticence. Maxim's demeanour up to and during his meeting with Pechorin suggests that he is not harbouring any hostility towards him over Bela. This would not have been clear to Pechorin, however, who might have attached some sinister motive to Maxim's persistence in seeking him out. A reason which, on the face of it, seems implausible, may, however, be the correct one in the context: speaking of Bela's death, in *Bela* Maxim tells us that '[Pechorin] Poor chap...was out of sorts for a long time and got very thin. But we never talked of Bela after that. I could see it would upset him, so what was the point?' (60). However, after an interval of some five years, might it not be possible for Maxim, who was deeply involved in the incident, and perhaps as fond in his own way of Bela as Pechorin was, to mention the death of Bela to Pechorin on the assumption that it had now fallen into some kind of perspective? When Pechorin thanks Maxim for not forgetting, Maxim replies angrily that he at least has forgotten nothing (70). He reads Pechorin's attitude to him as a sign of forgetting, just as, presumably, his own effusive response to Pechorin is a sign of the keenness of his remembering. Pechorin, however, has probably not sufficiently *forgotten* the Bela incident, a gap of five years notwithstanding, to allow him to share a memory with Maxim in the way the latter wishes. Maxim is not to know this; the reader too is not yet to understand it and must even suppose Maxim's apparent premise about the way Pechorin should now view this incident from his past to be a reasonable one given the nature of the time lapse. In this sense however, Pechorin is an interesting exception: '...I forget nothing, absolutely nothing' (105) he says in *Princess Mary* and 'moments of happiness one forgets, but sorrow never' (110).

. There is a mnemonic differential between the two men's attitude to their shared time together: 'Do you remember when we were at the fort together? Grand hunting country that! You were a keen shot too, weren't you? And do you remember Bela?' (70). What Maxim remembers of all this we know very well since he has told us at length. He is not able to tell us what Pechorin remembers; Pechorin himself will say nothing, and as Gregg points out (1984: 396) there is presumably no Journal account of the incident which might enlighten us. Pechorin is effectively silenced in terms of personal reaction to the Bela incident. Perhaps the denouement of *Princess Mary* had cured him of journal keeping for good, soon after arriving at the fort.

2.   The Role of the Narrator

Although in a sense Maxim Maximych 'owns' *Bela*, and Pechorin is reduced to the passive role of a narrated character, it is the Narrator who is the presiding genius in that story. Having heard *Bela,* he appropriates it in the last stage of a complex chain of emplotment: having 'overheard' Maxim narrating a plot which grew from the latter's own overhearing of an original plot by two Circassians. Just as the cynically superior intellect of Pechorin is able to make a 'yes' plot out of Kazbich's 'no' plot, so the Narrator will make a polished written plot out of Maxim's naive oral plot, something public out of something imparted privately. Maxim is a man of one story and has nothing more to tell: it is a lucky chance for the Narrator that Maxim has his heart broken by an unresponsive Pechorin whose Journal he gives away in chagrin. Reading it, however, the Narrator will discover that this is not mere chance. Rather it was Maxim's *mischance* to meet Pechorin again, for thus far he had turned out to be one of the few people to have become intimately involved with Pechorin and to escape unscathed. Thus far, indeed, he may be said to have done *well* out of Pechorin, entertaining travellers with his tales about him. By a strange twist of fate, however, he is brought to Vladikavkaz, together with a witness, to have a kind of public humiliation visited upon him. Does he deserve it? Perhaps it was inevitable and even right that he should not escape the spidery web of tribal vengeance which he was happy to construct in *Bela* and perhaps it is appropriate that it should be Pechorin who wreaks that vengeance and that what is enacted is a kind of anti-*kunachestvo*, a general severing of bonds. However Maxim cannot associate his treatment at the hands of Pechorin with any dereliction of duty on his own part towards his Circassian kunaks: 'I always knew he was flighty, of course, not the sort you can rely on. A pity he's got to come to a bad end, though. But it's bound to happen. As I've always said, no good ever comes of a man who forgets an old friend' (71). The irony of Maxim Maximych is in the relevance of his name to his behaviour and in his inability to apply to himself the 'maxim' which he rightly applies to Pechorin. This is the same failure of identification with Pechorin's vices for which Lermontov reproaches the reader in his Author's Preface. Pechorin, in bidding his last farewell in this story, takes Maxim down with him.[1] The reader will learn however that Maxim is not alone in his fate; he is remarkable only in that he is allowed a point of view. Otherwise, like Werner,

Grushnitsky, Bela and Vera, he receives a kind of condine punishment, one which perfectly reflects the nature of his association with Pechorin.

Knowing these things it is not surprising that the Narrator's attitude to him in *Maxim Maximych* should be subtly changed, to the extent that Barratt and Briggs are moved to ask whether this can be the same narrator who gave us the Maxim Maximych of *Bela* (Barratt and Briggs, 1989: 36). It could indeed be that Lermontov is playing with the excesses inherent in the *skaz* style here much as Gogol did in his Ukrainian stories, or more generally with the inherent contradictions of a narrating voice which has not foreseen the end of what it has begun to tell and is caught out, like a bad newspaper column, by the vagaries of its own changing opinions over time. The Narrator is happy to call Maxim a 'sterling fellow' in the story he is writing up in Vladikavkaz, little knowing or expecting that Maxim will shortly make his reappearance. Maxim was already beginning to bore towards the end of the joint journey to Kobi: 'I did not interrupt him, nor did I listen' (61). But this does not matter. As far as the writer knows the real, boring Maxim, the Maxim who has told his tale, has disappeared forever and only the Maxim of the story remains. The Narrator should not forget, however, that he is still writing 'not a story but travel notes' (45-6); the journal he will soon have thrust upon him will offer him a salutary example of the difficulty of making life run like a plot (*Princess Mary*), that of simple teleology: even with the vigilance and prescience of a Pechorin one cannot always predict what the end will be, so that real life turns its narrators into Monty Pythonesque Inquisitors constantly having to alter the structure of their discourse to accommodate unforeseen additions.

One interpretation of the Narrator's changed attitude to Maxim in *Maxim Maximych* is that it represents his real view of the staff captain, namely that he, unlike his story, is a bore. However this does not entirely account for the full gamut of stylistic changes which are evident in this story when compared with *Bela*. Turner is probably right in surmising that what we are meant to read into these changes is the influence of Pechorin's Journal on the Narrator's style (Turner, 1978: 14). As a general principle the *post factum* status of all the stories is anyway bound to be an important principle in their appreciation. Journal form, or narrative in Journal form, is common to both Pechorin's and the Narrator's discourse and it is precisely the retrospectivity or twenty/twenty vision acquired by these writers, whether Pechorin or the Narrator, which imparts inner consistency to their discourses. Only in *Princess Mary*, where true diary form is adopted, is this species of limited omniscience sacrificed and with it some of the consistency in Pechorin's view of himself. The acquisition of the Journal by the Narrator, however, is an intertextual event which we might reasonably assume to have had an impact on the style and attitude of the Narrator. The cynical view of how the reader may react to rapturous landscape descriptions (62), the more detached view of Maxim, already mentioned, and most of all the detailed physical description of Pechorin (which finds no parallel in the *Bela* account) all point to contamination by the style of the Journal. This is only to say, however, that Lermontov lets the Narrator echo elements of Pechorin's style which were not evident in *Bela*. We may also note, however, that the situation or setting itself is changed, from rural to urban in this instance, and it is also inevitably the case that certain features of plot structure are inherent in Lermontov's style (see below) and cannot be attributed to a fictional imitation of Pechorin by the Narrator. Such symptoms of influence between fictional styles suggest a preoccupation with poesis and intertextuality on Lermontov's part though, as Todd points out, not, as in *Eugene Onegin*, via the medium of a public readership (Todd, 1986: 145).

By the time that *Maxim Maximych* has been written up the Narrator will have almost certainly decided to publish Pechorin's Journal. In the original draft of *Maxim Maximych* the conclusion of the story actually contains the information that the Narrator intends to publish the Journal:

> I have looked through Pechorin's notes and have observed in certain passages that he had prepared them for print, in default of which I should not, of course, have decided to abuse the confidence of the staff captain. In fact Pechorin in some places addresses his readers; you will see this for yourself if what you know about him has not killed any desire you may have had to get to know him better. The notebooks were not numbered: some in all probability are lost because there is no great connection between them. But in spite of the bad example set by some journalists, I was unable to make up my mind to correct or complete somebody else's work: I have only changed one thing: I have put Pechorin in the place of his real name, which will not, of course, raise his ire against me. (Translation from Turner, 1978: 16)

The function of this concluding paragraph is, in the final version, fulfilled by a separate introduction to the Journal which makes Pechorin's death the pretext for publication rather than, as here, his having prepared the stories for print. The hiving off of this function into a separate and amplified section of the novel allows *Maxim Maximych* to stand more independently as a story and for Maxim's farewell to become an important emotional incident in the novel, the sad conclusion of *Maxim Maximych* contrasting with the 'major key', to use Boyd's phrase, in which *Bela* ends (Boyd, 1972: 36).

The Narrator is made to craft *Maxim Maximych* as a real story not a hybrid like his earlier effort. It has the crispness and consistency of *Taman* and indeed its style, tone and technique is such that we can imagine Pechorin himself having written it about other actants. Knowing what he does, the

Narrator must view matters with lofty detachment. In retrospect he must realise that all has been for the best since the Journal has fallen into good hands. The triangulation of characters in the story allows him to perceive both the protagonists from different angles. Yet he is not a wholly detached observer. Maxim's pain is made worse by the fact that not only is Pechorin snubbing him, but one who has heard his story about Pechorin is there to draw his own conclusions: 'He was clearly hurt by Pechorin's indifference, particularly as he had just been telling me what great friends they were and an hour ago had been sure Pechorin would rush to see him at the mere mention of his name' (66). There is something rather cold-blooded about this commentary, almost Pechorinesque in its penetration, and it is, of course, perfectly accurate. Barratt and Briggs detect something Dostoevskian in the mixture of sympathy and mockery which emanates from the Narrator in *Maxim Maximych* but it is perhaps simply the Olympian detachment of one who, having got what he wants, is not greatly concerned for the fate of the other players (Barratt and Briggs, 1989: 33-4).

There are also reasons why the Narrator's point of view, though super-ficially detached, should have changed subtly, between *Bela* and *Maxim Maximych*. Pechorin, however unique and individual, is likely to have more in common with the Narrator (who in earlier drafts of the novel was himself conceived as an army officer) a sophisticated Russian from the capital, than with Maxim. This has already been established in *Bela* in which the Narrator has been able to interpret Pechorin's views and attitudes sympathetically to a bemused Maxim Maximych. This affinity between the two seems to dawn upon Maxim in his grief: 'How can an ignorant old man like me keep up with the likes of you? You young city chaps, you're too stuck up. As long as you're down here, with Circassian bullets flying round you put up with the likes of me, but then meet us afterwards and won't as much as offer your hand' (72). At no time is any complicity between Pechorin and the Narrator hinted at but one wink or knowing look between Pechorin and the Narrator during his farewell with Maxim would have sufficed to tip the scales in this direction. As it is we have no idea how the Narrator comported himself during the embarrassing scene. He does however become the natural recipi-ent for reproaches, which, though they apply to Pechorin uniquely, Maxim now begins to realise, are symptomatic of a certain type of metropolitan officer. This also serves to make a definitive break between the Narrator and Maxim Maximych, for, although Maxim wishes him good luck, they 'said good-bye rather stiffly' (73). The Narrator, by a certain coolness towards Maxim which creeps in in the course of the story, as well as by his interest in the notebooks which Maxim has discarded, has edged himself closer to Pechorin with whom he anyway has a greater social affinity. Maxim has been enlightened to a remarkable degree: the whole incident, and possibly the presence of the Narrator, has enabled him to identify Pechorin's behaviour in social terms and broadly accurate ones at that. Yet the Journal will go further, showing Pechorin to be exceptionable, even among other stuck-up 'society chaps...down here with Circassian bullets flying around'.

3. The Portrait

Because of the fact that *Maxim Maximych* has generally been interpreted heterotelically in terms of the acquisition of Pechorin's notes, the elimination of Maxim Maximych and, most of all, the live appearance of Pechorin, much critical interest has focussed upon the nature of the portrait of the latter which is painted in the story. It is indeed a portrait, very much as if Pechorin had sat for it. However it is also the case that the close and prolonged scrutiny which the description implies is simply not consistent with the access to Pechorin which the Narrator, a total stranger, could have hoped to have had. This inconsistency has led Barratt and Briggs to suppose that Lermontov's aim was to discredit the portrait as a paradigm of realistic fictional characterisation (Barratt and Briggs, 1989: 89). Turner, among others, speculates that the Narrator is influenced in his portraiture by similar portraits in Pechorin's Journal and by the aesthetic principle which underlies them, namely that 'there's always some odd link between a person's outward appearance and his inner self...' (78) (Turner, 1978: 14-15).

It is certainly true that in Pechorin's (as opposed to the Narrator's) work, there are a number of prominent instances of this correlation being applied to human observation as well as significant examples of acts of scrutiny which (in contrast to *Maxim Maximych*), do not strain credulity. Of his encounter with the blind boy in *Taman* Pechorin writes: 'He stood before me without moving and I had a good look at his face...so I studied the blind boy's face...I took a long look at him...' (78). Before killing him in the duel Pechorin is given a chance to examine Grushnitsky minutely: 'For a few moments I stared him hard in the face to see if there were the least sign of remorse, but I got the impression he was suppressing a smile' (166); and in *The Fatalist*, before Vulich's trial of fate with the gun: 'I looked him hard in the eyes but he met my searching gaze with a look of steady calm and a smile flickered on his pale lips. Yet, for all his composure, I fancied I saw the mark of death on his pale face' (177).

All these instances of prolonged scrutiny are well motivated in the Eikhenbaumian sense: the blind boy unable to stare back in the usual way or to be affronted by a gaze he cannot see can be stared at ad lib.; the duel in *Princess Mary* has been arranged at the initially short distance of six paces (originally as a way of scaring Pechorin) and at Pechorin's request has been situated on the edge of a cliff. Grushnitsky, whose gun, unlike Pechorin's, is loaded, is concerned that his shot, which is to be the first, even if it only grazes Pechorin, will topple him over the cliff. He is therefore hesitating before firing, a circumstantially well-wrought pretext for the close examination described. The element of theatricality in *The Fatalist* episode is sufficient to allow Pechorin the opportunity of staring at the Serb without seeming out of place or rude. Even so, it seems significant that all three objects of this intense interest react to it by smiling – even, and somewhat eerily, the blind boy. These reactions on the part of three separate individuals do suggest that we are meant to take the *prolonged* staring literally in the case of Pechorin, i.e. he really was in the habit of staring at people and provoking an unnerved or embarrassed response. Of course, if we are content with a temporary *petitio principii*, we can use evidence from the portrait in *Maxim Maximych* to explain these responses, for we are told by the Narrator that when Pechorin looked at a person 'his quick penetrating sombre glance left you with the unpleasant feeling that you'd been asked a discreet question. It would have seemed insolent, if it had not been so calm and indifferent' (68).

From a semiotic point of view, then, Pechorin's eyes are not merely receiving in the usual way; they are encoding a message simultaneously and it is this which is being responded to by those he looks at. However we would not know that Pechorin's gaze had this effect if we were to rely on the evidence of his Journal alone since here the seeing Pechorin is a receptor of information about those he looks at rather than a sender. Of course the information sent by Pechorin's gaze is an impression; it is encoded by the receiver into an indiscreet question whether or not one was actively implied by the sender or not. A smile, however, since it has recognised semiotic status, is less ambiguous: it is both a response and an interpersonal message.

Such information as the above is vital for our full understanding of Pechorin's behaviour and clearly if the portrait in *Maxim Maximych* has simply been copied by the Narrator from instances of Pechorin's own portraiture in the Journal it cannot be used for this elucidatory purpose. Perhaps Pechorin, that great starer, has at last been outstared by the itinerant Narrator. If Pechorin's eyes 'never laughed when he laughed' (68) has the Narrator's intense scrutiny elicited a predictable response? The portrait is generally considered to be problematic because it is always assumed that the Narrator has, in effect, made him pose for it while smoking a cigar, sitting 'on the bench on the far side of the gate' (67). This is certainly what he is doing when the Narrator feels impelled to 'give a portrait of him' (67). However we will find that only a fragment of the whole portrait actually relates to that part of the Narrator's encounter with Pechorin which we may term 'the sitting': 'When Pechorin sat down on the bench his erect figure bent as though he hadn't a bone in his back. His whole posture gave the impression of nervous exhaustion. He sat in the manner of Balzac's *femme de trente ans*...' (67-8). The other features of the portrait, among them those which are most inconsistent with the nature and duration of the Narrator's observation of the seated Pechorin, could easily have been noted at leisure by him during Pechorin's discussion with Maxim before his departure.

We might therefore gloss the portrait as follows: 'On first seeing his face [when he came and sat on the bench] I would have thought him no older than twenty-three, though later [when he was talking to Maxim Maximych] I would have taken him for thirty...There was something childlike in the way he smiled [at Maxim]...only a prolonged scrutiny of his forehead revealed traces of criss-cross wrinkles [noted when he was talking to Maxim] that probably showed up much more in moments of anger or stress [he was not therefore angry or stressed during his encounter with Maxim Maximych].[2] His eyes 'didn't laugh when he laughed' [he laughed when talking to Maxim Maximych]. The portrait, then, is not at all implausible if it is considered as the distillation of the *whole experience* of the Narrator's encounter with Pechorin, using in particular the impressions gathered as a silent witness of the meeting between Pechorin and Maxim Maximych.[3] If Lermontov (through the Narrator) felt impelled to 'give a portrait' of Pechorin the reason may be one of creative pragmatism: a story which relies so much for its effect on the power of Pechorin's absence or non-appearance and of his hasty retreat, simply does not offer sufficient scope to motivate the description of Pechorin in any less formalised way.

All this is not to say that there are not important similarities between the descriptive methods used by the Narrator in *Maxim Maximych* and those used in Pechorin's Journal. The common principle is that of inferential characterisation which developed into an aesthetic absolutely central to Russian realism in the nineteenth century. The assumption was that from external indicators, facial expressions, complexion changes, as well as more permanent features, such as the eyes and facial proportions, it was possible to infer both transitory inner states and more permanent mental and psychic capacities. By corollary the realist writer could describe the unknowable inner depths of the personality and its moods by means of outward signs which soon become conventionalised. Thus, since blushing denotes shame, and blanching denotes shock, and trembling and fainting extreme shock, the frequency with which all these somatic phenomena occur in nineteenth-century literature may have more to do with literary semiotics than with the real pathology of people living in the nineteenth century. Helena Goscilo (1981) makes a compelling case for the origin of this aesthetic in the ideas of the eighteenth-century phrenologist Franz Gall and the physiognomist Johann Lavater, whose spurious psychological theories first linked by association the conformation of head and face to inner mental capacities. Goscilo also cites evidence for Lermontov's interest in these theories and it certainly does seem to be the case that in *A Hero of Our Time* Lermontov is not merely content to use outer-inner inference as a means of characterisation, but articulates the nature of the correspondence in theoretical or quasi-theoretical form.

However an examination of instances of the Lavaterian principle (if we may so describe it) in Pechorin's Journal shows us as many examples of its misapplication as of its successful implementation. The Narrator in *Maxim Maximych* is ready to admit that his portrait of Pechorin may have been prejudiced by the fact that he 'knew something' of Pechorin's life (68) and that 'possibly he would have made an entirely different impression on someone else' (68). Prejudice also seems to compromise the principle in *Taman*, for while Pechorin is ready to believe that there is a link 'between a person's outward appearance and his inner self' (78) he also admits that he is prejudiced against all people with deformities so that, in effect, he is always ready to read something bad into their expressions. However his contention that the loss of a limb or organ is likely to correspond to some loss of inner feeling also seems not to apply to the blind boy in *Taman*. Indeed his subsequent behaviour in *Taman* suggests a different theory, namely that of compensation: loss of a limb or faculty being compensated for by the hyper-development of others. Twice, in *Taman* and in *Princess Mary*, the same inferential process when applied to women is likened to the skilled appreciation of a horse, but in *Taman*, at least, Pechorin misjudges the points, searching for 'signs of madness' (84) in the smuggler girl's face, and misreading romantic motives into her unorthodox behaviour and speech.

Nakhapetov suggests that, from Pechorin's misreadings or misapplications of the Lavaterian principle, we should infer a deliberate intention by Lermontov to break the outer-inner correspondence. This is because, he thinks, if valid and rigorously applied, it would impose determinism on human psychology, for, if we could truly read people from their external characteristics, their motives and actions would become completely predictable to us (Nakhapetov, 1990: 95). Certainly it seems significant that the most complex and Pechorin-like character in the novel, Werner, is given close-cropped hair so that we can see 'the bumps of his skull, which would astonish a phrenologist by their strange mixture of opposing tendencies' (100). Clearly too the issue of determinism which Lavater raises is highly relevant to one of the novel's major themes: the relation of fate to free will. It is also true that the performative principle, as well as being a vital component of *Princess Mary*, is an integral part of Pechorin's view of the world, a world in which, to borrow the Jungian terminology favoured by Barratt and Briggs, characters adopt and hide behind personas which are often not their true selves, perhaps the direct opposite (Barratt and Briggs, 1989: passim).

4.   Structure and Structural Affinities

Maxim Maximych functions like a hinge between the double-authored *Bela* and the Journal. Accordingly it has three themes: the fate of Maxim Maximych, the physical Pechorin, and Pechorin's notes. The orientation of the story is however pro- rather then retro-spective. Pechorin's refusal to share with Maxim Maximych more than a few valedictory moments means that it is impossible for the story to amplify on their common past. Pechorin's remarkable passivity in the story also leaves us little for the present, apart from the still life of his portrait. The portrait of Pechorin offered by the Narrator both does and does not make its subject present to us (rather like the celebrated portrait in Shakespeare's first edition with its epigraph warning us to 'look not at his portrait but at his book'). In his 'book' alone lies any future development of Pechorin as a character; Pechorin the physical presence, like his old friend Maxim, reaches vanishing point at the end of *Maxim Maximych*.

However the prospectiveness of *Maxim Maximych* is something of a cunning artifice. Mersereau is right to point out the peculiar affinities which *Maxim Maximych* has with the story which precedes it:

> *Maxim Maximych* is not a complete short story, for its whole meaning and importance depend upon its contiguity to *Bela*, since without the knowledge of the relationship between the captain and Pechorin revealed in that story, there would be virtually no significance to their encounter in Vladikavkaz. Nor is it simply a sequel to *Bela*, for, from the point of view of form, *Bela* ends much more logically without such a pendant as *Maxim Maximych*. (1962: 97)

Mersereau is correct on all these counts but he has not fully developed the implications of his arguments. What he is saying, in effect, is that, while *Maxim Maximych* implies the *Bela* story, the latter does not imply, and indeed would be better without *Maxim Maximych* since it stands in need of no sequel. However *Maxim Maximych* is not just a sequel to *Bela*; it is in effect the same literary entity, since there is an almost seamless line of progression linking the events of *Bela* with those of *Maxim Maximych*. Together they comprise the Narrator-authored part of the novel and moreover the only genuine travel notes. The travelogue begins with the Narrator's chance encounter with Maxim Maximych and ends with his final farewell to him. The hiatus introduced by the Narrator's temporary separation from Maxim is in fact negligible in terms of time and distance: 'After leaving Maximych I travelled briskly through the Terek and Daryal gorges, lunched at Kazbek, had tea at Lars and arrived in Vladikavkaz in time for supper...I put up in a hotel...my first day was very tedious...early next morning a cart drove into the yard, and who should it be but Maxim Maximych!' (62). Two nights have elapsed since the Narrator last saw Maxim Maximych. Despite this, however, the epilogue of *Bela* tries to show that the parting between Maxim and the Narrator at Kobi was meant to be definitive: 'We never expected to meet again, but in fact we did' (61). We are asked to dwell upon the virtues of Maxim Maximych as though this 'meeting again' were not going to impinge upon our overall assessment of him. It is not so much therefore, as Mersereau contends, that *Bela*'s ending is good enough on its own: *Bela* has to end in the way it does *in order* to differentiate it as a discrete textual entity from *Maxim Maximych*. The changes in the Narrator's attitude both to the landscape and to Maxim Maximych serve the same purpose; a distinct stylistic regime will operate in *Maxim Maximych* in which dialogue will be suppressed, Maxim will be silenced ('We sat in silence. What was there to talk about?' [63]) and the Narrator will operate less, as previously, as listener and interrogator, than as, virtually, a non-participative first person narrator. The changes can possibly be explained as a kind of stylistic osmosis with the Journal which has already been touched on in a different context and the structural implications of which we will examine shortly.

However it is worth asking why, if *Bela* and *Maxim Maximych* really do comprise a single organic whole, it becomes necessary so starkly to differentiate them both in style and genre. The answer is almost certainly that, were the two stories conflated into a single seamless narrative, with no pretext given for a definitive separation, however brief, between Maxim and the Narrator, the events in the latter part of such a single story, in Vladikavkaz, would seem so preposterously coincidental as to subvert its plot. This is simply because we measure the plausibility of coincidences in terms of the number of opportunities available for them to happen and we consider a coincidence rare or unlikely if there are many more chances of its not happening than of its occurring (this is why Vulich's survival seems so remarkable in *The Fatalist*). By disrupting the continuum of the Narrator's dialogue with Maxim Maximych Lermontov allows the *Bela* story to drift into the past and creates the illusion of a separate unrelated incident and 'if you like I'll tell you about it. It's quite a story'(61). That all three men (Narrator, Maxim, Pechorin) might meet up somewhere, some day, is not as implausible as would be the sudden unmotivated appearance of Pechorin immediately after the staff captain has been telling a story about him; and it is precisely such a plausible discrete chronotope which *Maxim Maximych* seeks to set up.

In its structure *Maxim Maximych* has clear affinities with the storied sections of Pechorin's Journal: *Taman* and *The Fatalist*. In the novel as first conceived the Journal consisted only of *Princess Mary* and so, curiously, *Maxim Maximych* would have been the only orthodoxly structured story in a collection of three. Although structurally quite distinct, it has affinities with *Taman* in which Pechorin, is, like the Narrator, detained unwillingly, in a provincial town. In both stories the protagonist's curiosity produces a tragic denouement in which illusions are shattered. It shares some similarities too with *The Fatalist* particularly in point of Pechorin's role as observer and ultimately actant: the Narrator too observes, but finally intervenes by appropriating the Journal. In this appropriation, a kind of opportunistic flash of inspiration, the Narrator mimics similar acts of opportunism by Pechorin. Just as Pechorin takes up and acts upon the proposal which Kazbich has refused in *Bela*, so the Narrator uses Pechorin's refusal to repossess the notebooks as a chance to acquire and ultimately to publish them. This suggests a pre-existing affinity between

Pechorin and the Narrator which seems to intensify in the Foreword to the Journal, for it must be borne in mind that the writer of *Maxim Maximych* can be presumed himself to have read the Journal before writing it.

The story *Maxim Maximych* ensures that Maxim will occupy a unique place among the characters of *A Hero of Our Time*. One commentator considers him, next to Pechorin, the most interesting character in the novel (Sengupta, 1984: 25). This is reflected in a critical tendency exemplified by Lotman (1985) of dividing the society of the novel up into a number of discrete identity categories, one of which is represented by Maxim Maximych.[4] There is no doubt that much of the interest and complexity of Maxim Maximych derives from his social and ethnic ambiguity which is emulated but not surpassed by the bored Pechorin. The brief resuscitations of Maxim Maximych in Pechorin's Journal (*Princess Mary* and *The Fatalist*) serve to keep him alive as a measure of 'Caucasianism' while Pechorin pursues a different course of cultural assimilation in the region.

Notes

1. Richard Gregg sees 'the farewell' as an important motif in the novel as a whole. In particular he isolates Pechorin's 'four gestures of denial' which are: 1) his ceasing to keep a diary (a farewell to himself); 2) his treatment of Maxim Maximych (a farewell to his fellow man); 3) his leaving Russia to go to Persia (a farewell to his native land); 4) his death (a farewell to life itself). See Richard Gregg, (1984: 389).

2. Significantly the meeting also 'ages' Maxim Maximych who though only fifty, calls himself, and is called by the Narrator (for the first time in their encounter) an 'old man' after the meeting with Pechorin has finished. However, it should be noted that Maxim's 'old man's silliness' on p.42 of the Penguin translation is a gratuitous addition by the translator.

3. See Gorelov (1984: 77-80) on the preponderance of gestures and non-verbal signs in Pechorin's leave-taking.

4. Since this is the most rudimentary way of taxonomising the novel's characters many critics have indulged in it, but there is some variation in the way the characters are classified: Lotman (1985: 12) has 1. Maxim Maximych; 2. Spa society; 3. Pechorin. A.N. Sokolov (1965: 801-2) has something similar but groups Maxim Maximych with the Circassians. An early English writer, Charles Edward Turner (1882: 352) suggests 1. The Circassians; 2. Maxim Maximych; 3. Pechorin plus Grushnitsky, Mary, Vera and other members of civilised society.

Taman

1. A Problem of Belonging

According to the best authorities *Taman* was probably drafted in 1837 and is therefore the first of the constituent stories in *A Hero of Our Time* to have been written (Udodov, 1981: 108). It was first published separately in 1840 when, however, it was accompanied by an editorial note to the effect that it was 'another exerpt from the notes of Pechorin, the hero of the *Bela* story' (e.g. Turner, 1978: 23). These circumstances have led some commentators (e.g. W.E. Brown, 1986: 245-6) to assume that it was not conceived or written to have any connection with the Pechorin of the novel, a view supported, or at least not refuted, by the fact that Pechorin's name is not used in the story. Its inclusion in the novel, the original core of which consisted of *Bela*, *Maxim Maximych* and *Princess Mary*, must therefore be associated with the same process which inducted *The Fatalist* into the novel, a desire on Lermontov's part to diversify the contents of Pechorin's Journal by adding more free-standing narrative to the explicitly 'diaristic' structure of *Princess Mary*. *The Fatalist*, however, has Pechorin addressed by name and a short reference to Maxim Maximych at the conclusion which therefore inscribes it formally into the context of the novel.

Clearly the introduction of such inter-referential material was one way open to Lermontov to incorporate a self-standing story into the overall structure of the novel. The other way was simply to collocate the story alongside others supposed to have come from Pechorin's pen. We might say that this process took place with *Taman* the moment it was published in the *Notes of the Fatherland* with an allusion to the pre-existing published account of Pechorin's adventures (*Bela*). Apart from this, the location of the individual stories in the novel as a whole, the order, that is, in which the reader encounters them, creates its own Gestalt much in the manner of a collage. *Taman*, in entering the final published version of the novel was made room for by *The Fatalist* which had, until then, occupied the position between *Maxim Maximych* and *Princess Mary*. The arrival of *Taman* therefore had the effect of relocating *The Fatalist* into the terminal and therefore potentially epilogic and explicatory position which has been responsible for a good deal of the critical debate about its role (or otherwise) as the key to the novel. *Taman*'s position likewise has inspired lines of interpretation based on the nature of the unfolding character of Pechorin, of which the most influential, in Anglo-American criticism at least, has been that of Richard Peace (Peace, 1967: 12-29).

In fact, of course, Gestalt-based interpretation is the only way in which we can discuss the place or role of this story in the novel, since Lermontov has made no other referential concessions within the text itself. Yet it is also the case that this lack of reference to Pechorin or his Journal, or to anything else which takes place outside *Taman* in the novel, is well motivated by the setting and context of *Taman* itself. Pechorin is a stranger in Taman and there is no-one to call him by name, his Cossack batman being reduced to a soporific ineffectiveness. Also, since *Taman* is supposed to represent the earliest phase of Pechorin's sojourn in the Caucasus, there are as yet no other characters (like Maxim in *The Fatalist*) to whom reference can be made. There is nothing, either, in the way the story is written to suggest that it belongs to a journal: quite the contrary. We only know that it belongs in a journal by organic inference, or structural Gestalt (or form): through the simple fact that it has been included in the Journal. Inna Arian's polemical reply to Peace's article (1968: 22-32) is largely concerned with this matter: the point about *Taman*, she argues, is that it proves that Pechorin is a creative writer, an artist, and, as an artist, he reveals himself through his work in *Taman*, no less than in *Princess Mary* and *The Fatalist*. This argument appears to run counter to the accepted view (developed by Peace) that there is a progression through the novel towards ever greater revelation of Pechorin's character. However Arian's view, if taken to its logical conclusion, makes the inclusion of such a work as *Taman* in a journal highly problematical. Arian associates its presence there (and presumably, that of *The Fatalist* also) with the fact that Pechorin was a writer *who did not wish to publish*; privacy, presumably being a defining quality of the diary or journal genre. However, as our previous discussion of *Maxim Maximych* showed, at an earlier stage in the creative history of the novel Lermontov was content to motivate the publication of the Journal by the fact that its author had clearly prepared some parts of it for publication. The paradox of *Taman* is that, being originally an autotelic story, its contextualisation in *A Hero of Our Time* makes it subject to interpretations which may run counter to those appropriate to it when taken in isolation. By a mere sleight of hand it is transformed from a free-standing tale into a revealing chapter in a private psychological history; without undergoing any changes in its own textual identity it has crossed from one form of discourse to another.

In recent years there has been a tendency to treat *Taman* in isolation from the rest of the novel. However since it is difficult to account for *Taman* fully, in terms of its genre and preoccupations, without reference in particular to romantic conventions and precedence, we may find (as in Zholkovsky's recent study [1992: 248-56]) it being compared to such stories as *Bela* outside the framework of the novel, that is alongside other works of similar romantic preoccupation, such as *The Gipsies, Poor Lisa, The Water Nymph*. Even apart from this, critics attempting an autotelic reading of the story may ultimately have to have recourse to a heterotelic interpretation in order to provide a metatextual closure.[1] Gilroy's general point about *A Hero of Our Time*'s problematising the ownership of the text (Gilroy, 1989: 18) is particularly relevant to *Taman*. Even if, as it seems, we have every critical justification in treating *Taman* as an autonomous text without reference to the novel as a whole, we find it difficult to wilfully deny ourselves such a helpful context, its co-textual contrasts and comparisons, particularly in the case of a story like *Taman* which deliberately mystifies both in plot and in relation to the hero's identity. It is this mysteriousness which ensures that, thus trapped in the greater structure of the novel, *Taman* will not readily be allowed to escape. What distinguishes *Taman* from the other constituent stories of the novel is not merely that it alone is capable of standing separately, but that this capacity must inevitably create an interpretative tension between the two readings, the independent and the integrated, the auto- and heterotelic. In the study which follows an autotelic reading will be attempted, a reading based on what we can legitimately derive from the story if we take it in isolation from the novel. This will be followed by a heterotelic approach which will provide an infusion of interpretative perspectives germane to the novel as a whole. These two approaches, it is hoped, fairly correspond to the relation of *Taman* both 'to itself' and to the novel as a whole.

2. An Autotelic Reading

To deny oneself the hermeneutic support of the rest of the novel is to be thrown into something of the mystery and confusion which faces the story's narrator. Andrew is right to identify blindness as the dominant theme of the story (1992: 449-76): embodied in the blind boy, it is also a metaphor for the itinerant officer's condition throughout *Taman*, where lack of vision, according to deep-structured etymological assonance, also signifies lack of knowledge.

Since the story is narrated in the first person we know that it has been written after the event, for first person narrative, with all its epistemological shortcomings, has survival inscribed into it. These two features of first person narrative (epistemological restriction and survival) are indeed exploited to the utmost in the action of the story, for, from the hero's point of view, it is powered by his need to overcome initial epistemological restrictions, deliberately, as it turns out, engineered by those with whom he comes into contact; and, of course, as he reveals in the opening lines, he was nearly (but necessarily not completely) drowned. In that the first person voice is the voice of survival, it enforces the comic (or life-affirming) principle at the expense of the tragic, at least so far as the protagonist is concerned.

We are not given much more guidance by its narrator as to how to read the story (see Ripp, 1977: 979); if there is any wisdom in his hindsight the narrator does not reveal the benefit of it at crucial points in the work. He

comes to us as a travelling officer with prejudices about the disabled and
views on women based on his reading of Goethe and coloured by an ironic
eugenics. Neither of these theoretical postulates stands the test in what turn
out to be the extraordinary exceptions of a miraculously well-compensated
blind boy and an apparently unsophisticated girl who has from somewhere
managed to obtain the full template of the contemporary male romantic's
sexual fantasies. Our narrating voice, however, does not tell us whether he
has abandoned these preconceptions or whether their overturn in *Taman* was
a freak accident.

The restraint on the use of retrospectively derived information for
lectorial guidance may be what Chekhov admired in the story. Chekhov's
professed love for the work has become a critical enigma, for there are so
many ways in which *Taman* may be thought of as 'Chekhovian'. However
the matter is of some relevance since *Taman* appealed to Chekhov as a
perfect example of the short story genre (in itself, that is, and certainly not
as the component of a novel). Eikhenbaum speculates that Chekhov was
attracted precisely by the limitations of *Taman*: unlike, for instance, *The
Tales of Belkin*, its excellence does not lie in its being a novel *in nuce*, but
specifically in the fact that it is an incident developed artistically to the
utmost of its potential (Eikhenbaum, 1981: 169). Zholkovsky, on the other
hand, feels that it may have been the breakdown in communication, the
confusion of codes between the hero and smugglers, which struck a familiar
chord with the later writer (Zholkovsky, 1992: 254). Chekhov, then, albeit
rather vaguely, underwrites an approach to *Taman* which valorises it as a
short story *per* and *in se*. The interpretation of the story under these
conditions has to be undertaken in the context of the totality of the experiences of both the smugglers and the travelling narrator as a complex
semiotic episode. The lives of a group of smugglers have been changed
forever by the inept interference of one over-curious army officer who
though initially distressed by what he has done ('I felt sad. Why did fate
toss me into the peaceful midst of these *honest smugglers*?' [90]) is able to
reach a kind of callous indifference to what has happened, suggestive of
closure through oblivion. In such a reading the weeping blind boy becomes
a small icon of life's indiscriminate cruelty, like the similarly weeping boy
at the end of Turgenev's *Singers*: the story is concluded by absorption into
the universal. All this is a far cry from the heterotelic interpretation which
has to identify the narrator as Pechorin and grapple with the rhetorical use
of the word 'fate' in terms of a greater determinism evident throughout the
novel as a whole.

In fact an autotelic reading of the story allows us to account for the nature
and causes of the events in *Taman* in terms of the ignorance of the narrator
and the relative cunning and intelligence of the smugglers. Brown, one of
a minority of critics who works on the assumption that *Taman* is not
necessarily about Pechorin, is therefore able to say of its narrator (but not

of Pechorin) that 'he is not very bright' (Brown, 1986: 246) and deserves to be drowned. This, however, does not seem to be the point of the story. The hero's prejudices and preconceptions, already mentioned, are not peculiar evidence of his stupidity, but are rather attitudinal features intended to be recognisable to the contemporary reader. The itinerant officer is an every-man within the given social context and, without our being able to substitute ourselves for him in the matter of his curiosity, we as readers would not be able to participate sympathetically in the fear and suspense which he undergoes, and on which so much of the story's effect depends. It is ignorance rather than stupidity which is the defining feature of the narrator of *Taman* and he is thus a representative of the reader's ignorance in the face of the strange and uncanny events which unfold in the work. Furthermore the narrator's ignorance is revealed as such by the fact that in the end the uncanny elements of the story are shown to have a rational explanation.

Taman, then, read alone, is about the limits of our understanding when confronted by a mysterious Other. When this Other is finally understood it is found to centre on a group of subversive individuals living on the margins of civilisation, alien to the author and his military calling. The story contrives to make this group of people both admirable and sympathetic and it is precisely their manipulation of the uncanny which enables them to appear in this light. They have managed to subvert and confuse the very things which give metropolitan man, the representative of law and empire, his superiority – culture, education, in a word, greater *knowledge* – by enmeshing him in the toils of ignorance. They reverse the Hegelian socio-epistemological order whereby (unhappy) consciousness resides with the lord and productive ignorance with the servant. In *Taman* the educated western man of the mid-nineteenth century experiences the frontiers of his knowledge, appropriately enough in a port on the edge of the Russian empire. In accordance with the dominance of the binary theme of knowledge/ignorance epistemic and logical devices essential to traditional western knowledge are put to the test and are found wanting in *Taman*. Most noticeably the story is made to establish the setting entirely by means of negatives and privatives. The narrator knocks on the door of his would-be lodging: there is no answer. He calls for the master of the house and is answered not by the master but by a boy. He is told that there is no master. There is a mistress, but she is not here. He asks who will open the door, but the door opens by itself (i.e. 'nobody' opens the door); he lights a match to see the boy and to be seen in turn, but is confronted instead by blind eyes, a visual 'no'. A blind boy, as it were, puts a face to this dialectic of negativity but such a face can provide no positive information to the narrator: 'What can you expect to see in a face without eyes?' (78)

The narrator next has recourse to his 'Lavaterian' theory, a contemporary diagnostic technique aimed at deducing the essential inner by means of the outer. But he himself has already formulated it in the negative. For the Lavaterian principle, from the outer sign to the inner signified, the narrator has substituted 'from the loss of the outer sign, read the loss of the inner signified'.[2] If this is not quite the stupidity detected by Brown, it is certainly suspect logic: it is incorrect to infer, from the erasure of the sign, the erasure too of the signified since the semiotics of the Lavaterian process read the inner from the outer, not the outer from the inner. For, since the inner is perceptible only through the outer, it cannot be verified as absent merely by the absence of the outer.

However it is not merely that the narrator's theory is logically flawed. The blind boy is quick to prove this to him empirically. Counter-adaptation has made him as agile and sensitive to outside impressions as any sighted person. When he first begins to suspect this the narrator reports it in a rhetoric designed to heighten its unnaturalness and uncanniness: '...suddenly the "ghost" of a smile "flitted" across his thin lips. For some reason this struck me very unpleasantly. I had an idea that this blind boy might not be so blind as he seemed' (78). At this stage the narrator seems to intend these words literally for he adds that rationally he knew that 'there was no way of faking wall-eyes' (78). In fact, however, he will soon have to accept the truth of the situation, at the price of his previous theories: that the blind boy has developed superior sensory skills which enable him to function like a sighted person. When the Cossack finally provides him and us with confirmation that the boy is both blind and capable ('He goes everywhere on his own, fetches the water, goes down to the market for bread...' [82]) the narrator appears to grow angry: 'Well, what of it?' (82).

The blind boy not only challenges the scientific preconceptions of the narrator, however, he also threatens to cross what might have been thought the unbridgeable chasm between the empowered and the disempowered which is central to ensuring the normative epistemological and social structure. The received power dynamics which should place the narrator, Russian, educated, an officer, sighted, mature, *over* (in an Adlerian sense) the provincial (Ukrainian) ignorant, civilian, blind juvenile, is being challenged in this one instance and, by a principle of *pars pro toto*, the narrator comes to fear that in Taman *all* is uncanny, mysterious, or, in the Cossack's words *nechisto* (unclean). The unnatural and frightening in *Taman* are intimately related to the empowerment of the conventionally disempowered, a process which develops in the story to involve the blind boy's mother and the girl, as we shall see.

The litany of negatives and privatives continues beyond the speculation that the blind boy might not really be blind. Since he has learned nothing, but has rather been deprived of what he once thought was a valued way of knowing, the narrator continues to receive only negative signs which signify to him only the absence of a signified: he is not the son of the house, he is an orphan (no parents), the woman has no children, her daughter has gone, with a Tatar whom 'I don't know' (79). Even the hut is described in a negative vein: no furniture, no icon. Interestingly enough such a preponderance of negatives in no way hinders the aesthetic effectiveness of the story. In the case of the furniture, for instance, they serve a positive function of indicating what the narrator would consider the corresponding positive attributes to be: a hut *with* furniture and icon presumably. The same is true of his questions to the boy. Answered in the positive they would create a full and coherent profile of a family, a predictable social group with whom the narrator could have dealings. In this way too epistemic status implicates social predictability.

The search for knowledge is the most consistent feature in the activity of the narrator both mental and physical. It is wrong, for instance, to interpret his venturing out on to the cliff simply as an impulsive act of reckless curiosity. This action is merely one component in a single epistemological urge which informs his questioning of the blind boy, his appraisal of the hut (sc. why is there no furniture; why is there no icon?) and his inability to sleep because of the blind boy's sphinx-like image rising before him in the darkness. The cliff face which both the narrator and the blind boy descend is an ideal device for measuring the dynamic differential between the two figures. The man is above and the boy is below, as befits the orthodox power scheme, but the man is following him downwards and in his descent is less sure than the boy is. Although the conversation which follows introduces another important character into the action – the girl – she remains a disembodied voice and the scene serves to complete the characterisation of the gifted blind boy who now speaks in pure Russian and who is able to detect the approach of the boat by hearing in the dark when both the sighted persons present (the girl and the narrator) can make out nothing either by sight or hearing. The sensory stakes have now been raised: two pairs of eyes and ears, eight organs of perception, are inferior to the blind boy's two. By this calculus the normal rules of epistemological dynamics are definitively turned on their head. The blind can 'see' more effectively than the sighted. The boy's bilinguality, too, perhaps related to his keen ear, gives him a communicational advantage over the narrator, who, of course, is still unable to interpret the signs which he has overseen and overheard.

After this episode the narrator makes a brief visit to a neighbouring fort to find out when he can take a boat out of Taman: 'But, alas, the commandant couldn't give a definite answer'. Forced by such a negative answer to return to his lodgings in Taman the narrator participates in a curious reprise of his first arrival at the hut, his interlocutor this time being the Cossack. Once more negatives abound: 'It looks bad', says the Cossack, the place is 'unwholesome' (82); a sergeant he knows says that the 'people are a bad lot' (82) and then he himself proceeds to dilate on the gifts of the blind boy. Otherwise, however, this episode promises superficially to answer the questions which went unanswered or received negatives the first time. 'Has the woman come back?' asks the narrator (82). Yes. She has her daughter with her too. On entering the hut, though, the narrator finds as much to mystify him as to enlighten. The meal which was being cooked 'looked rather lavish for poor folk' (82) and this contributes to the disorienting impression of social irrationality and non-specificity. The old woman, it turns out (almost comically) is deaf. Finally this scene achieves almost full symmetry with the first in a second interview with the blind boy complete with questions and inevitable denials: he didn't go anywhere last night. He wasn't carrying a bundle.

There is no doubt that *Taman*, though it is meant to create an atmosphere of mystery and confusion, is very clearly structured. Barratt and Briggs have isolated five distinct moments in the narrative based on the various comings and goings of the narrator to and from his hut (Barratt and Briggs, 1989: 60); both Andrew (1992: 449-76) and Zholkovsky (1992: 248-56) have sought to impose the Formalist distinction of fabula and sujet on the story, however in rather different ways. For Zholkovsky the fabula is the conventionally romantic apparatus of the story (the mystery, exoticness etc.) whereas the sujet is the way in which these are realistically deflated (the squalidness, the robbery by the blind boy, the fight with the girl). Andrew almost inverts this precedence, regarding fabula as that which the smugglers are actually doing and sujet as the mysterious gloss put on these actions by the romantically inclined narrator. In fact both of these approaches deal with the single phenomenon of the narrator's ignorance of the truth of events, with Zholkovsky stressing the showing up of his ignorance and Andrew the nature of the ignorance itself. However, it is arguably quite difficult to apply the fabula/sujet distinction to this story because the author's ignorance and illusions (about the girl) are not something distinct from the facts but play a dynamic role in the real order of events.

The most important structural moment in the work is that determined by characterisation. The dialectic of endless repetition involving the blind boy and the revelation of his empowerment is abruptly supplanted by the appearance of the girl, so far prefigured only by her disembodied voice. The trajectory of the narrator's involvement with the smuggler girl runs parallel in so many ways to that of his encounter with the blind boy that it can be regarded as a symmetrical part two of the story, separated from the blind boy episode by the narrator's musings about Petersburg, the cultural predilections of which city the encounter with the girl will curiously exploit. As the narrator was confronted by a socially disempowered (because juvenile and disabled) boy before, so he is confronted by a girl who is young, but old enough to be sexually attractive to him. It may be of some significance that he first encounters her above him, whereas presumably he had first looked *down* into the face of the boy which he illuminated with a match: a foretokening of her future power relationship to him. The narrator subjects her to a similar preliminary scrutiny to that received by the blind boy although, unlike him, she is able to suggest her empowerment not despite, but through her returned gaze which possesses 'magnetic power' (84).

As with the blind boy the narrator is able to bring to bear on her preconceptions of a positivist nature relating to good breeding and in addition his reading of Goethe which allows him to characterise her as his water-nymph or 'ondine'. The mysteriousness of the girl is not, as in the case of the blind boy associated with negativity, but rather with riddle and enigma and on a broader behavioural level with'...sudden changes of mood, from restless activity to complete inertia...enigmatic speeches...skipping...strange songs' (85). And in the absence of the negative mood which dominates his dealings with the boy, the application of the Lavaterian principle is somewhat different. Where, in the first case, we had an absence of signs, here we have a hypertrophy of signs both visual and vocal. This abundance of signs will mislead the narrator just as much as the blind boy's dearth of them, for just as the inner may exist without being signified by the outer, outer signifiers may bear a misleading relationship (or none) to the inner. Signification without inner correspondence is, of course, a characteristic of performance and this is what the narrator is treated to by his ondine. His mistake is not to recognise it for what it is. He fails to realise that performance holds a position midway between fiction and reality and that when he sees his favourite fiction imitated in life this must be called performance, not reality. He does, however, succumb to what is another example of the inversion of the epistemological order: representation usurping reality.

The ondine's answers to the narrator's questions, though they are not in the negative, give him no more information than those of the blind boy. Hers is a different form of non-informative response: it stresses the semiotic validity of the message together with the receiver's inability to decode it. Thus the girl says of her singing: 'It'll be heard by the one it's meant for, and you won't understand if you are not meant to hear' (85) and of what the narrator claims to have seen on the beach: 'It's plenty you saw, but little you know' (86). Between them the boy and girl confront the narrator with the two basic forms of ignorance: not knowing and not understanding.

Zholkovsky suggests that both the narrator and the smugglers operate within mutually incomprehensible codes and misread one another's activities and intentions in terms of their own codes (Zholkovky, 1992: 253). Thus the narrator reads the girl in what Zholkovsky terms the 'Don Juan' code – as a seducible young woman – and she reads him in her smuggler's code as a spy. Both also play up their roles for each other. This may well be the reason why the narrator rashly warned the girl that he would report what he had seen to the garrison commander, something which he 'later had occasion to regret' (86). What is more important, however, is that he does not connect the mysterious phenomena going on around him with what he has seen on the beach, and thus does not realise that he is being treated to a performance. His thought process is paratactic rather than syntagmatic: not 'they are doing *a* because of *b*' but 'they are doing *a* and *b* both of which constitute a mysterious *c*'. This is an epistemological weakness on the narrator's part.

The ondine however must have grasped the nature of his thought processes. She must realise that, though he suspects what she is, he does not suspect her performance. This at least is the valid inference if we consider that her subsequent attempted seduction of the narrator is in effect a continuation and intensification of the previous performance. This is a performance of a different order. Her previous role was as a decoy and she quits it appropriately in bird-like fashion: 'With a sudden hop...she burst into song and vanished like a bird startled from a bush' (86). It was an end in itself, its aim being to mislead. The seductive performance is subject to a teleology, the narrator will be invited out into a boat and drowned. The second performance works because it offers something to the narrator, uniquely among all his encounters in *Taman*, promising him fulfilment, albeit not intellectual.

It has, of course, been noted in many different contexts that the narrator is unmanned in his struggle with the girl. It exemplifies in a final and conclusive way the power inversion which informs the whole narrative, and its relation to lack of knowledge, since the narrator finds himself in this position through misreading and ignorance. Female seduction contains the key to the power inversion which operates in the story: it is not merely a case of female initiative taken where it would not conventionally be anticipated; it is the manipulation of the expectation of domination which enables the dominated to dominate, the socially inferior to become superior. In knowing that the narrator will come if she offers herself, the ondine is epistemologically empowered since she knows what he will do but he does not know what she will do.

We have here something close to the Hegelian dialectic of transcendent consciousness. However in that transcendence the retrospective first person narrator, the survivor by definition, will ultimately transcend the consciousness of his attacker, for he now knows that she knew that he did not know what was going to happen to him when he accompanied her to the boat. His is that unhappy consciousness which Hegel located at the end of the process of mutual cognisance: the rueful possessor of a sort of enlightenment. Within the narrative itself, however, the ondine triumphs by her sublime intelligence. The blind Wunderkind is left to grieve on the beach and his mother soon to die. His mental powers, like the girl's, have been wrought out of a deficit and disempowerment but the departure of the girl and Yanko drop him back into perspective. He is neither mature nor genuinely mobile; his wonderful agility works only in the place in which he has been born. The departure of Yanko and the ondine disclose this disablement. This too must be a salutary revelation to the narrator. However in our autotelic reading this narrator disappears forever; we will never know what he does with the potential insights his experiences may have given him; after his narrating voice is silenced, only the reader is left to supply a final stage to the transcendental process of anagnorisis (or recognition) which underlies *Taman*.

3. A Heterotelic Reading

The case is very different if we make *Taman*'s travelling narrator Pechorin and read the story intertextually against the other components of *A Hero of Our Time*. Under these circumstances we will find that an intertextual interpretation will legitimately intrude at virtually every structural level which critical interpretation is capable of isolating. Both the identity of the narrator and of the other actants, confined to mystery and uncertainty in an autotelic reading, become susceptible to amplification. Although, for instance, the story gives some clue to the ethnicity of the smugglers (the location of *Taman* on the Black Sea, the use of Ukrainian, the name Yanko, even, as Barratt and Briggs have suggested, the absence of icons suggesting a muslim influence [Barratt and Briggs, 1989: 53] something to which Black Sea Cossacks, like Pechorin's batman, in their staunch orthodoxy would be peculiarly sensitive) we are now able to locate this story alongside the other primitive settings which the novel offers us and to situate it more reliably within an ethnographic model. Utilising, too, our knowledge of the supposed chronology of Pechorin's route into the Caucasus, and of its topography, we may wish to regard the setting of *Taman* in a Saidian sense, as a topos located at a point in Pechorin's journey from the centre, Petersburg, to the periphery of the Caucasus, a place more uncivilised than Russia, but not yet the full-blown romantic barbarism of Bela's Chechnya. Russian is still spoken, though so is Ukrainian, and the prominent role of Cossacks suggests that we are on the Russian side of a line dividing us from the barbarians. At the same time however this is a far less civilised place than the fashionable Piatigorsk which will be Pechorin's next port of call: as Andrew (1992) has suggested, it is the liminality of the location which is striking.

The sea in *Taman* provides a romantic setting with the same potential for activating romantic notions of primal freedom as the hills of Chechnya. Nevertheless the smugglers' assertion of freedom, though it is like that of the Circassians against Russian imperial power (and against Pechorin as its representative) is arguably *intra*-national, carried on by Slavs against their own Slavic state and is thus sharply differentiated from the *inter*-national struggle waged by Circassian abreks like Kazbich. Within the context of the novel, then, the smugglers fall into the general category of 'primitive' and are thus marked by the recurrence of the words 'dirty' and 'unclean' which the novel's narrator and Maxim Maximych use also of Ossetians and other Caucasian aborigines. The childishness, or at least youthfulness, of all the participants in *Taman* also feeds into the themes of primitiveness and disempowerment inasmuch as the child may function as the ontogenetic symbol of a phylogenetic primitiveness.[3] Up to and including *Taman* the victims of Pechorin's activities in the widest sense have all been representatives of ethnic groups closer to the primitive than the civilised: Bela and the Chechens, Maxim Maximych (the near-naturalised Caucasian) and the smugglers; among the smugglers, however, only the blind boy promises, like Maxim Maximych, to be a lasting victim, or, put another way, and less flatteringly to the hero, a blind boy was Pechorin's first victim in the South.

At the other extreme a young woman can now be numbered alongside Kazbich as one of the few who have managed to transcend ethnic or sexual disempowerment and faced up to Pechorin. Critics taking a feminist or gender-oriented approach to *Taman* have shown how the ondine and her behaviour fit into the general pattern of the treatment of women evident in the novel. Both Barbara Heldt (1987) and Joe Andrew (1992) underline that Pechorin creates in the girl what he wishes to see, a process which he takes further in his treatment of the eponymous Princess Mary. His treatment of her bears out what Andrew elsewhere believes to be the deeply mysoginistic treatment of women which informs the whole novel (1988: 53). Certainly if *Taman* is read against both *Bela* and *Princess Mary* the conclusion may be reached that the treatment of the ondine is very much in character for him.[4]

Although our interpretation, amplified by the context of the novel, moves forward in the confidence that the hero of the story is Pechorin, we are also in a position to read its voice against that of the novel's Narrator in *Bela* and *Maxim Maximych*. Turner (1978: 23), for instance, thinks that the style of *Taman* is close to that of the Narrator since 'it lacks...the penchant for introspection which is so much in evidence in *Princess Mary* and *The Fatalist*'. We may add too that in *Bela* as much as in *Taman* information deficit is a prime motivator of plot although the narrator's inquisition of Maxim Maximych, leading to his acquisition of the Bela story, is more successful than Pechorin's general interrogations of the inhabitants of Taman. The Narrator of *Bela*, like that of *Taman*, was originally meant to be an itinerant army officer and both narrators may be presumed to be new to the South (at least, the general critical consensus is that Taman is Pechorin's first port of call on his way to the South).

While (as in an autotelic reading) the narrator remains anonymous, we have no way of knowing whether there is meant to be a time lapse between the adventure and its writing, or, if there is, whether this can be made to have any significance when we have nothing more than a disembodied authorial voice. However, since we know that Pechorin's world view alters significantly in the course of his *chronological* progression through the novel we may, as Turner suggests, conclude that 'since what we see here is a younger Pechorin, a less practised player in the game of skill that he makes of his life, and a less analytical introvert...the best that the later Pechorin could make of the incident was to poeticise it' (Turner, 1978: 24). Such a reading would certainly account for the remarkable mixture of moods which comprise the epilogue of the story: an initial statement of sadness and regret in the pre-penultimate paragraph immediately after the blind boy is left sobbing on the beach; a return to a narrative coda in the penultimate paragraph with the bathetic revelation that Pechorin's valuables have been stolen and the rueful reflection that he has been 'robbed by a blind boy and very nearly drowned by a girl of eighteen' (90); the definitive farewell of the last paragraph in which the narrator is now able to view the whole Taman episode with an almost carefree detachment.

Such questions of poesis and auto-redaction lead on also to the matter of the story's aesthetic status. Despite Brown's view that it would have been better left out of the novel (Brown, 1986: 46) we have to contend with Chekhov's already quoted valorisation of it and the fact that it has sometimes been thought of as proof of Pechorin's artistic mastery. Arian's argument (1968: 22-32) is that if Pechorin is writing a *story* in *Taman* then we have no more right to identify the narrative voice (and hence the protagonist) with its author (Pechorin) than we have in the case of any fictional work, or, closer to home, we should make only the same kind of identification between the hero of *Taman* and its author, as between the hero of *A Hero of Our Time* and its author Lermontov. Such a view, however, reduces Pechorin, in *Taman* at least, to a sort of phantom, a fictional character who has written a story in the first person but about whom we may not infer anything from the story itself. It also assumes that it is not possible to write a strongly autobiographical story. Nevertheless we would have to agree with the view that the kinds of rhetorical subterfuge used in *Taman*, for instance in the conclusion, must be of an essentially literary nature and that it and *The Fatalist* are undoubtedly *stories* despite their inclusion in a journal.

Since *Taman, The Fatalist* and *Maxim Maximych are* stories it is also legitimate to explore the structural affinities between them, even though *Maxim Maximych* itself is authored not by Pechorin but by the Narrator. Both *Taman* and *Maxim Maximych* share a common setting which enforces an unwanted delay on a travelling officer just arrived in a small town (in drafts, it will be remembered, the Narrator was indeed an officer). This enforces a common unity of place, time and theme in the two stories. However the Narrator's wait in *Maxim Maximych* is soon supplanted by Maxim's own private drama of expectation, whereas in *Taman* the expectational theme is quickly obscured by the mystery of the setting. In both stories, as suggested above, Pechorin's victims are left distressed at closure. Freeborn calls *Taman* a bridge between the two discrete parts of the novel (1973: 56) but the liminality of setting which is a prominent feature of both stories, suggests that there are two such bridges (Garrard uses the phrase 'breathing space' [1982: 136]) in the novel, one (*Maxim Maximych*) leading out of the travel notes into the publicistic discourse of the Narrator (the Foreword) and the other (*Taman*) leading into the Journal.[5] This functional similarity between the two works is highlighted by the fact that there are few if any structural affinities between *Taman* and *The Fatalist*.

By contrast there are a number of quite distinct areas of common ground between *Taman* and *Bela*, most of which have been catalogued by Richard Peace (1967: 27-8). Among these are character parallels (Kazbich=Yanko;

Bela=Ondine; Azamat=blind boy); functional parallels (Pechorin steals a horse to give to Azamat; the blind boy steals from Pechorin to give to Yanko); and plot parallels: Pechorin lures away Bela; the ondine lures away Pechorin. These parallels, unlike those between *Taman* and *Maxim Maximych*, do not relate to the structural function of the stories in the novel. Rather they suggest a reworking of certain interpersonal patterns. Whereas Kazbich loses his horse to Pechorin and only possesses the heroine by killing her in an act of revenge, Kazbich's double in *Taman* (Yanko) goes off happily with a heroine who is never possessed by Pechorin. And whereas Azamat is able to benefit by Kazbich's misfortune in *Bela*, his double in *Taman*, the blind boy, is left bereft at the conclusion. The inversion of the abduction of the heroine by Pechorin is, however, the key to this parallelism. As Barratt and Briggs point out, the girl, in being associated via Goethe with a water-sprite, becomes in effect the *rusalka* of Russian folklore, 'a creature of vengeance, the dead spirit of a seduced and drowned young girl who appears at night to lure a man, sometimes, but not necessarily, her erstwhile seducer, to a watery grave' (Barratt and Briggs, 1989: 55). *Bela*, in particular, leaves a tangled web of unrequited wrongs, particularly in relation to the abduction and death of Bela, and Pechorin, sufficiently familiar with the Caucasus to have known the dangers of becoming enmeshed in such actions, appears to walk away scot-free. It is appropriate therefore that, in the first story of the Journal, Bela's logical double should appear to exact her revenge, although in purely chrono-logical terms this produces the interesting paradox of a revenge being exacted in advance, something, however, rendered plausible under conditions of strict predestination and divine prescience.[6] In this way *Taman*'s preoccupations reach not only back to *Bela* but forward to *The Fatalist*.[7] Zholkovsky, however, takes a different view of the ondine's role: the conclusion of the story leaves the ondine worse off for her encounter with Pechorin, notwith-standing the fact that she has tried to drown him, since she is forced to leave her home forever (Zholkovsky, 1992: 251). This, argues Zholkovsky, con-trasts with the general romantic convention adhered to in works as disparate as *The Gipsies, Bela, Poor Lisa,* and *Eugene Onegin* in which the hero is not allowed to escape emotionally unscathed from his role in the heroine's unhappiness or tragic fate. This deviation from the norm is part of the story's project to deconstruct romantic convention.

The two readings of *Taman* offered above illustrate the considerable correspondences between the story and the rest of the novel. This could perhaps be taken as something close to empirical proof (if this is still needed) that the novel is indeed an organic whole. Nevertheless it should still be borne in mind that *Taman* offers its reader no explicit association with the name of Pechorin. It forms what Koffka and other Gestalt psychologists termed 'good Gestalt' with the rest of the novel; that is, once juxtaposed with the other stories it will be found to have more features which suggest that it forms a whole with them, than suggest that it should be regarded as a separate entity. This is a potent receptional principle, not necessarily limited to the anonymous hero of *Taman*. The hero of the three stories which comprise the Journal acts and thinks in each of them in very different ways. Yet since we understand this to be one, and not three heroes, we explain these differences in terms of psychological complexity and thus, as readers, contribute to the contradictoriness of Pechorin's character.

Notes

1. Andrew's study exemplifies this (Andrew, 1992: 449-76), for his essentially gender-based close reading concludes as a polemical reappraisal of Richard Peace's view of the collapse of Pechorin in *Taman* (Peace, 1967: 12-29).

2. For the influence of Lavater on Lermontov, see Goscilo (1981: 500-15).

3. On this see Peter France (1985: 298). I adapt these terms from their original biological senses, which are respectively the development of an individual organism and the development of an entire group of organisms.

4. Axelrod (1993: 115) traces this misogyny to the loss of his mother by Lermontov – 'object loss' – which makes him both anxious for female love and hostile (since woman represents that which deserted him in childhood).

5. For more on the novel's structural symmetry and repetitions see Rowe (1979: 35).

6. If we are certainly going to commit some wrong, and if wrongs are certainly punished by God who knows all things in advance, then it is not illogical for us to be punished for such wrongs in advance.

7. Freeborn indeed regards revenge as the principal theme of the novel (1973: 38).

Princess Mary

1. Diary and Drama

Princess Mary is often regarded as the core of *A Hero of Our Time* and much of the discussion of the enigma of Pechorin's character over the last hundred and fifty years has in effect centred upon the statements which Pechorin makes about himself in *Princess Mary*. Historically there is some justification in giving it this central status. As the novel was first conceived Pechorin's Journal *was Princess Mary* and, of course, its diary form makes it seem to be essentially what the Narrator's introduction promises us, which is not the case with the stories *Taman* and *The Fatalist*. Moreover *Princess Mary* is the longest component of the novel and so, on a crude quantitative criterion, is likely to 'tell us more' than any of the other stories individually. *Princess Mary* has, despite its diary form, often been treated as if it were a novel in itself and one important part of the critical heritage, as we shall see, has been devoted to comparing it to other nineteenth-century Russian novels. Paradoxically indeed, if regarded as a novel, it is more thematically conventional and far less structurally problematical than *A Hero of Our Time* itself.

Because of its diary form, however, there has been a general assumption on the part of critics that by definition it must be more psychologically informative about Pechorin than the stories which precede it in the novel. A tendency in recent years, however, has been to question this accepted view. Among Soviet critics we can find this scepticism in Grigoryan's approach to the novel as a whole. Things get less, not more clear for the reader as it proceeds, he thinks: 'Reticence makes its appearance, mysteriousness and intimations that words may have hidden meanings...' (Grigoryan, 1975: 209-10). He associates this partly with increased dramatisation, an important feature of *Princess Mary*'s plot, which we shall discuss later; partly too (and this is typical of his rather unorthodox views on Lermontov for the time and place of writing) it is a symptom of romantic (rather than realist) style since such mystification is more generally associated with romaniticism. By contrast another prominent Soviet Lermontov critic, Fokht, defended the more conventional view that *Princess Mary* is less of a romantic work than *Taman* and *Bela* because in it Pechorin is associated with people from his own civilised milieu and not with exotic tribes of the Caucasus (this however assumes a rather narrow identification of romantic with exotic [Fokht, 1963: 580-1]).[1]

Turner notes the fact that 'although Pechorin's self-analyses have frequently been taken at their face value...they are not so helpful as at first sight they appear to be' (Turner, 1978: 30). This view has been generally followed in studies by Gilroy and Barratt and Briggs, the latter extending scepticism about literal readings of *Princess Mary* to include characterisation too: Grushnitsky, they point out, is often treated as though he were a character out of the works of Turgenev or Tolstoy whereas, since he is mediated to us only by Pechorin, we should be prepared for a highly subjective portrayal.

Reflections such as these have underlain the increase in sceptical, ironic, rhetorical or broadly postmodernistic readings of the novel as a whole among contemporary critics, as though Lermontov, which may be the case, deliberately intended us to be deprived of a definitive view on his hero or his thoughts. However our conclusion need not be so extreme. Finishing his portrait of Pechorin in *Maxim Maximych* the Narrator observes that it may indeed be subjective, but that 'as you will hear nothing of Pechorin except from me you must be content with the picture I give you' (68). This kind of pragmatic acceptance of the inevitability of partiality may be a more reliable guide to how we should read Pechorin on Pechorin and others than the more extreme forms of ludic scepticising which have sometimes been put forward in recent years.

Crucial to the question of psychological veracity and inner revelation is the semiotic status of the diary as a medium of communication. Yet even the latter predication is problematic since it is not at all clear with whom diaries are meant to communicate. It is precisely this question which the narrator addresses in the Foreword to Pechorin's Journal when he assumes that a journal's honesty depends on whether it was intended for publication or not ('the trouble with Rousseau's Confessions is that he read them to his friends' [75]). In earlier drafts of the novel Pechorin, as we have already noted, was supposed to have prepared his notes for publication, and, even if this is *formally* not the case in the final version of the novel, the Journal does seem to consist of two kinds of work: *Taman* and *The Fatalist* which, since they are stories, imply possible publication and *Princess Mary* which, as a diary, does not immediately suggest a public readership.

In fact the publicistic status of a diary is highly ambiguous: it is a fact of cultural history that diaries *are* published and sometimes, as a result, become established as celebrated bellettristic or even literary works. Indeed, if diaries were primarily secret acts, they and their discourse would never have entered the public domain as a recognised genre. In fact the reverse is so. We know, and Lermontov's readers would have known, both from classic examples in the confessional mode like Rousseau's *Confessions*, as well as from fictionalised diaries as vehicles for narrative, exactly what the *public* norm for a diary is. In the same way they, like us, would know, in the case of Gogol's *Diary of a Madman* precisely how and where Poprishchin's document departs hilariously from the accepted template. The sign of genuine privacy is concealment. In *Bela* Maxim Maximych, baffled at Pechorin's long explication of his unfortunate character which could well have fitted into an entry to his journal, asks the Narrator whether Pechorin was typical of all the younger generation. The Narrator replies, in effect, that he is broadly typical although '...now the people who suffered most from boredom tried to keep their misfortune to themselves, as if it were some vice' (54). The suggestion is that there has been some change in the attitudes and behaviour of the bored Byronic type since Maxim first made his contact with it some six years before. It was then more public and performative; it has with the years grown more solitary and secretive. We may even infer from the Narrator's remarks that the Pechorins of this world have learnt to keep their thoughts to themselves and themselves to themselves, a lesson which *Maxim Maximych* may be showing us that Pechorin has learnt.

The diary, then, is a sufficiently established genre to have a broadly accepted and recognisable form. This form, moreover, enforces certain stylistic restrictions peculiar to the genre (as well as allowing particular liberties). Diaries often have a stated reason for beginning when they do but the reason for their discontinuation can only be surmised. In a fictional context some motivation for starting the diary may need to be articulated by way of exposition in order to establish for the reader its range, purpose and scope. In the case of *Princess Mary* we are led to believe that we are at the end of a date-structured journal since *Princess Mary* is prefixed by the subtitle 'The end of Pechorin's Journal'. This could of course simply be an explication of the 'Part Two' which was a pragmatic editorial intrusion into the second edition of the novel. It could be, on the other hand, that 'I arrived at Piatigorsk...' (91) signals the opening of a diary and its implied motivation: Pechorin's adventures in Piatigorsk. Since Pechorin strains every nerve to organise a complex adventure in Piatigorsk this is not an implausible inter-pretation. According to such an interpretation Pechorin comes to the spa prepared to keep a diary of his adventures there. These adventures he conceives in essentially dramatic form so that the diary becomes an intertext or even a synaesthetic artifact: Pechorin translates his drama into diary form.

The endings of diaries, arising, as they often do, from extra-textual causes, are often not signalled intra-textually. Diaries must have a fixed beginning (or they would not exist) but have no prescribed ending. The termination of a diary, moreover, signals something of a diminution of the psychic self-knowledge which its composer enjoyed while he or she was keeping it. Above all, some change of circumstances overtakes the diarist which renders his or her life unrecordable and often for that reason such change is not recorded. In the same way the day-logged journal of Pechorin, that is the diary proper, ends without explanation before the duel with Grushnitsky, and although Pechorin, now at the fort some six weeks later, promises to 'go on with my journal that's been interrupted by so many strange events' (157) it is a different kind of document which he offers us: a story rather than a diary with a formal epilogue based on a maritime metaphor which recalls *Taman*. Why has the diary *qua* diary come to a halt? We are not told. We can infer, however, that some change in Pechorin's life has intervened, such as to make it no longer inscribable in diary form, a change most likely connected with the duel in Piatigorsk. All of this suggests to us both the advantages and limitations of the diary to Pechorin as a mnemonic, artistic and epistemic tool.

The diary also has fairly clear temporal and gnoseological parameters so far as its author is concerned. A temporal feature, pointed out by Sollertinsky, originally in connection with *Maxim Maximych* (see above) but applicable to all the stories in *A Hero of Our Time*, is particularly relevant to *Princess Mary*. As we noted in the case of *Taman* the retrospection of the first person narrator will necessarily deform the true nature of events, producing a mnemonic sujetisation of fabula (Sollertinsky, 1973: 77). The recollecting 'I' has the benefit of a known outcome to events which is denied to the experiencing 'I' who, in the written account, is made to act as though the outcome is still in the balance. Thus, paradoxically, such a writer conceals his knowledge of closure in order to describe the temporary ignorance of his earlier self. In a diary, however, this can never completely be so. Since, as we have seen, the diary is not a discourse which inherently implies closure (since this is enforced on it extra-structurally) its writer will never be able to gain the omniscient privilege of a definitive closure to the diagetic process he or she has been recording. There will instead be a series of conditional closures – the individual entries themselves – which may be short or long time segments, depending on the date of the last diary entry, but which are forced to affirm temporary or conditional closure at the moment of writing the last entry.

Pechorin's diary runs over thirty-seven days between 11 May and 16 June. In fact less than half of these days (17) have separate entries. Those days which are not recorded are not in any sense lost days; they are, however, relatively uneventful, so that, when uneventful days occur or accumulate, the diarist waits until either they become cumulatively significant or their non-eventfulness becomes significant in itself. Thus there is a lapse of five days between the second and the third entry of *Princess Mary* which, when it comes, is short and records irritatedly that 'nearly a week has gone by and I still haven't met the Ligovskys' (116). On the other hand the first entry, which records only 11 May and the preceding day, is several pages long and allows Pechorin to record all the main actors in his drama and to set his stage. There are clusters of entries for consecutive days suggesting the dynamic development of events. But there are also lapses (e.g. between 23 and 29 May) which are accounted for not by a dearth of events or stagnation but by the satisfactory and unimpeded progress of Pechorin's plans. Date inclusion is therefore very much an arbitrary decision of the diarist and it is the significance of its incidents which determines the inclusion of a given day and not, as in a ship's log, the day which determines the record of incidents. This choice of dates is of course ultimately a fiction; through Pechorin's voice Lermontov uses the diary as a flexible medium, its entries as arbitrary sectionalisations akin to paragraphs. However the epistemic restriction has to be observed even by a fictional diarist, who unlike a retrospective narrator, *non respicit finem*.

Since he does not have end-knowledge, the diarist must resign himself to endlessness. This is generally what happens in real life: the diarist is guided by the principle 'sufficient unto the day'. The fictional diary, however, is in a different situation. It is in effect a story masquerading as a diary. As *Princess Mary*'s author, Lermontov knows that the work must end in such and such a way, with the death of Grushnitsky, the spurning of Princess Mary and so on. However since this story is mediated via the diary of its protagonist, the dialogue between the voice of immediate participation and the voice of retrospection, normally inherent in first person narrative, is silenced; the voice of retrospection is entirely suppressed. For Pechorin as protagonist no story exists beyond a given day of entry, but this is a fiction: all the entries have been written and each successive entry contributes to a terminal voice which, in the epilogue, will comment on them all.

Although the suppression of a foreknown future is central to *Princess Mary*, the teleological or prospective demands of plot are supplied by the hero's own artistic concerns and personal fantasies. Where in conventional retrospective first person narrative the plot is shaped both by what the protagonist is doing at any point and what he or she knows retrospectively, in *Princess Mary* the plot is structured out of what the hero knows at any particular time and what he hopes, wills and demands should happen prospectively. The nature of the diary medium not only motivates but nearly demands this: in recording the most recent stage in a current course of events the diarist can either speculate about its outcome or actively seek to determine it. This produces a double voicing in diary discourse which is akin to that in retrospective first person narration though in a restricted and conditional sense. The moment of writing represents the juncture between the recorded past and the emergent future. Whereas the retrospective first person narrator looks back from the narrating present into the completed past, the diarist looks into a yet to be written future out of a present comprised both of the moment of writing and of the recent past he is writing about.

From this it follows that the fictional diarist, Pechorin, if he is to fulfil what is an essentially fictional function – to keep a diary which has already been 'written' for him by Lermontov – must will a future which has already been fixed for him, though he is ignorant of it. He cannot therefore help but act in the way he is shown. He must strive to create a drama out of a group of people whom he appears arbitrarily to have picked for his dramatis personae; he must attempt to elicit as much information as he can, to ensure that his plot is not overturned. He must watch out for unscripted events. Thus, for instance, the duel appears not to have been part of his plot, which, though it had from the start involved Grushnitsky, was meant initially to function simply as an amorous triangle. The arrival of Vera and the duel are in fact extraneous to Pechorin's plans but he manages to incorporate them into his intrigue as though they were part of the original plot. Ultimately, of course, it does not matter which events were planned by Pechorin and which were totally contingent: Pechorin is as fictitious a character as all the rest in *Princess Mary* and his struggle to create a drama out of these different kinds of event is merely the artistic conceit through which Lermontov chooses to unfold a plot, which, aside from the singularity of its narrator and his chosen form, is a fairly typical society tale. The collapse of the diary form into pure narrative at the end of *Princess Mary* is of course well motivated but it is also a laying bare, the removal of an artifice: the logic of narrative was there all along beneath the apparent spontaneity of the diary.

The diachrony of the diary form enforces an inevitable psychic doubling.[2] The diary makes it easy for the writer to construct himself as an Other whom he can examine like a separate person. Although some of the reflections which Pechorin makes about himself in the diary of *Princess Mary* have analogues outside it (his remarks to Princess Mary in the June 3 entry, for instance, are similar to those made to Maxim after the death of Bela) they have to be carefully motivated in advance by the creation of highly charged emotional situations which will justify Pechorin speaking in such a way. In the diary however Pechorin can give free rein to such reflections with himself as auditor while the psychological analysis extended to the other characters goes well beyond what was possible under the constraints of conventional narrative fiction.

The diary, then, permits the representation of both self and others in forms which would not be possible outside its covers and it thus disrupts the normal hierarchic distinction between self and others by permitting both to be analysed in the same way. This accounts for the prominence of doubling in the characterisation system of *Princess Mary*, a feature often commented on. The emergence of Grushnitsky as a double figure of Pechorin depends largely on our being able to perceive Pechorin as clearly as Pechorin himself perceives Grushnitsky. The diary context is uniquely suited to fulfil this descriptive function. The same is true of Werner, who reflects many of Pechorin's own inner qualities. Since Werner and Pechorin scarcely communicate on profound matters 'and know practically all the other's innermost thoughts' (101) how else is the reader to obtain such information about Werner? The diary democratises the ego by making both

writer and written alike into scriptive characters (see Kesler, 1990: 497) and
in this way, not only, as Barratt and Briggs say, do other characters become
'dynamic elements in the mental life of the hero' (Barratt and Briggs, 1989:
77) but both diarist-hero and characters can be seen as constituting one
scripted reflection of reality. The diary then, in itself, prompts and encour-
ages Pechorin to regard both himself and those he meets in real life as
simultaneously participants in a scriptive universe, and from this it is but
a short way to a *scripted* universe.

Gilroy very perceptively notes that the undermining of 'the reader's
sense of the distinction between art and reality' (1989: 43) in *Princess Mary*
represents the initial stage of a phenomenon which would be taken much
further in the twentieth century in the visual media of film and television.
The diary alone is not sufficient to permit Pechorin to effect his identification
of art with life. The diary performs its alchemy secretly. Only a performative
medium is capable of representing the common scriptedness of self and
others in visual reality. Hence at the point where Pechorin begins to realise
the wishes he articulates in his diary he moves into another, the performative
medium. Yet both diary and drama together form an organic whole: a drama
scripted in diary form for performance in real life. A variant of this hybrid
genre has been familiar to us for some fifty years in the audio-visual media:
what is conceived in *Princess Mary* is indeed a serial, if not a soap, a narrative straining for closure in a medium which denies it.

The aesthetics of the diary-drama of *Princess Mary* are however more
complex than those of such contemporary popular genres. Pechorin first
conceived his idea of a drama in conversation with Werner ('The stage is
set', I cried, delighted, 'we'll see if we can provide a *dénouement* for this
comedy' [102-3]) and then recorded it in journal form. From now on all the
elements in the drama would be performed and then recorded in the Journal.
This process goes side by side with continuing plans to develop the drama
as a prospective task ('I want him [Grushnitsky] to pick me as his confidant
– then I'll have some fun!' [109]).

Just as the diary democratises the hierarchy between self and others (self
becoming just one more scriptive Other) so a diary-drama erases the hierarchy
between author and actor, script and performance. Although Turner insists
that 'as an actor in his own comedy, Pechorin is not able to write the whole
of the script' (1978: 53) this seems to suggest too rigid a definition of drama
to reflect what is happening in *Princess Mary*.[3] Indeed, better metaphors
can be found: Gilroy suggests that Pechorin's role:

> resembles that of the buffo in Italian commedia dell'arte and
> used by Schlegel to describe his idea of transcendental
> buffoonery. The buffo or harlequin character directs the plot
> and mocks the action at the same time. He interrupts the play

to make comments to the audience and although he may destroy the illusion he also motivates events (Gilroy, 1989: 44).

Todd uses a cognate, though distinct character metaphor, that of the masquerade 'a special type of performance in which participants were at once actors and spectators' (1986: 153). Both of these dramatic genres suggest a conflation of aesthetic functions which are normally kept separate: the harlequinade – that between actor and author; the masquerade – that between audience and actor. In the case of *Princess Mary* we will find Pechorin regularly taking all three roles. Not only this, but the entire story has about it an atmosphere of performance (as Todd suggests) since so many incidents (be it Mary picking up Grushnitsky's glass, or being insulted at the ball, or Pechorin luring away Mary's admirers by his scintillating conversation) have in place the basic conditions for dramatic integrity: actors, an act, an audience. Todd (1986: 156) implies that society itself may be responsible for the scripted nature of these set pieces. Since spa society, as much as the primitive society of *Bela*, enforces a highly predictable code for human interaction it is possible to regard it as in many ways pre-scripted before it is formally scripted by Pechorin. When Pechorin announces that 'the stage is set' and that there is 'a plot', this is conventionally interpreted as applying primarily to his own creative intentions, as though Mary, Grushnitsky, Vera etc. are transformed into fictional characters purely in Pechorin's imagination. In fact, given such people, such a place (a spa), such ritualised social mores, involving, for instance, the exposure of marriageable young women to eligible army officers and the exposure of jealous young officers with a strict code of honour to one another, quasi-dramatic and ritualised incidents may be predicted with a fair degree of accuracy.

It may be argued that such cultural phenomena are dramatic only metaphorically, but there is no doubt that performance in its widest sense, as a distinct form of semiotic cultural activity, is now a recognised way of defining social interaction. The fact that much social activity can be interpreted in terms of role and performance would suggest that drama, uniquely among literary forms, is capable of interpreting and clarifying interpersonal relations, rather than just fictionalising them.[4] The more traditional view, therefore, of Pechorin's attempt to dramatise real life in *Princess Mary* may now be inadequate. Drama, far from distorting real behaviour, or, in its enforcement of roles, as Turner suggests, promoting inauthentic behaviour, really does reflect the way individuals interact in real life. It may be, that, like Grushnitsky, they adopt a role which, from another's point of view (Pechorin's), is inauthentic, but this does not mean that Grushnitsky is any less Grushnitsky when he is performing, any more than John Gielgud is any less John Gielgud when he is playing King Lear. In a Wittgensteinian sense people can only be *known* performatively and Pechorin's activities in *Princess Mary* merely lay bare this fact. Turner seems to come somewhere close to this view, though grudgingly perhaps, when he speaks of modern man in general as:

> an inveterate actor whether as a result of direct social pressures or through the agency of the Freudian superego...and we no longer know where the role ends and the authentic person begins. This loss of self-hood is as commonplace as is the attribution to it of many of the tensions and schizophrenias of contemporary society. But it is a pattern of which Pechorin, with his aggression, his divided self and, not least, his role playing, is a patent exemplar (1978: 54).

Barratt and Briggs approach the Pechorin of *Princess Mary* in a similar way, armed, however, with Jungian rather than Freudian psychology. Here (Barratt and Briggs, 1989: 67) role is replaced by 'persona inflation' whereby the ego becomes over-associated with the persona and other parts of the psyche are neglected. As a result Pechorin's behaviour becomes 'pathological'. As with Turner's approach this assumes performers to be inauthentic even though their actions are real. If, for instance, it is not the 'real' Pechorin, but his persona which quips in French with Grushnitsky, performs a Circassian horse display for Princess Mary, puts on a witty performance for the local dandies, who else can it be? It seems an unnecessary complication to have to assume buried depths beneath role plays when it is quite sufficient to say simply that that is what characters are doing: playing a role. In the case of Barratt and Briggs, moreover, the assumption of a split between the role (persona) and an unknown real character beneath or within inevitably draws in the whole cast of Jungian figures which supposedly dwell beneath the persona and these roles then have to be distributed among the characters of the story (Grushnitsky as the shadow; Vera as the anima) in a manner almost as fantastic as Pechorin's own dramatic fantasies.

It seems more realistic to concentrate on the phenomenology of the role play itself and on Pechorin's consummate versatility in this regard. It may very well be that if we indeed *are* our roles, then those who can play many roles to many audiences are more effective *selves* than those who play only a single role like Werner, or play badly like Grushnitsky. This perhaps is what Pechorin means (even if the terminology is different) when he says that the form of ideas is action (performance): 'The most active man is the one who conceives most ideas, and so a genius stuck in an office chair must either die or go mad, and, in the same way, a man of strong physique who leads a sedentary and temperate life will die of apoplexy' (127). According to such a scheme individual effectiveness is not determined by whether the individual is ego or merely persona or, in

Turner's terminology, self or role (false divisions as I have suggested) but rather by the number of roles he or she can play and by his or her expertise in executing them. This is an adaptive view of human capability of the sort which evoked admiration from the Narrator when he found the relevant qualities in Maxim Maximych: 'I couldn't help being struck by the capacities of Russians to adapt themselves to the ways of people's they happen to live among. I don't know if this is a praiseworthy quality or not, but it does show wonderful flexibility...' [43] (something which the unfortunate staff-captain loses at the end of *Maxim Maximych*).

Ethnicity is precisely such an area in which versatility of role can be displayed. Pechorin's ability to pass for a Circassian makes him more effective than Grushnitsky, who does not attempt such a feat since this is one more role available to Pechorin in his performance to Princess Mary which is unavailable to Grushnitsky. On the other hand the Pechorin of *Taman* is outwitted by more competent role players than he. He has learnt something since then. As Lotman points out Pechorin is many different things to the various individuals he comes into contact with (1977: 45): a strange person, a villain, a vampire, an outsider, a true love, a decent fellow, a wandering officer. We may see this as evidence of his abundance of roles, though, as Lotman notes, it is also evidence of the large audience before which Pechorin is allowed to play these roles. Pechorin is put among those who, in general, are less flexible than he in this respect; but who is to say whether a Grushnitsky, a Princess Mary or even a Kazbich will not go on to have as many roles elsewhere?

2. Intra-textual Affinities

The diary form serves very well to mask the structural affinities which *Princess Mary* has with the other stories in the novel; yet these exist. If we strip it down to its basic plot we will find that it has general morphological affinities with *Bela*. In both stories Pechorin seeks to abduct/seduce a young woman by means of intrigue with the help of a complaisant confederate or confidant (Maxim Maximych; Werner). Both of these characters are socially undetermined (a Caucasian and a *raznochinets*) and the fact that he has to use such a type twice in the capacity of co-adjutor says something about Pechorin's isolation from his own class and social milieu. In each story Pechorin faces a rival from the same social group to which the woman he wishes to possess belongs. The comparison thus offered between Grushnitsky and Kazbich in this role is unfavourable to the former and is one of the ways in which spa society and the metropolitan Russian society of which it is a microcosm is exposed to subtle ridicule when *Princess Mary* is read against the other story. Interestingly the nexus of events in *Bela* makes Kazbich not a rival of Pechorin but an enemy: he relates to Pechorin via difference rather than, as in the case of Grushnitsky, by a despised similarity which tells us much about Pechorin's own inner conflict.

In both stories the confidant receives full, detailed and sympathetic characterisation as an unusual and worthwhile character; yet in quite different ways their singular psychological traits serve to bring them into a situation of non-communication with Pechorin – Maxim by his failure to understand him, Werner by his ability to understand too well. Despite this, both men part with Pechorin in the same way: one wishing to embrace him, the other to shake hands, and Pechorin refusing to do either. In the case of Maxim Maximych the death of Bela has come between them; in the case of Werner that of Grushnitsky. In *Princess Mary* the male rival dies, the death connived at by Werner who was second in the duel. In *Bela* the rival Kazbich gets away scot-free and, as we showed earlier, his virtual indestructibility is strongly brought out. In *Princess Mary* the heroine escapes with her life. In *Bela* she does not and her lingering death is presided over by Werner's counterpart Maxim Maximych. Both these male figures, then, are deeply implicated in the deaths which dominate their respective stories.

Bela is followed by *Maxim Maximych* which, as I suggested earlier, is in many ways the conclusion of the same story despite its structural independence. The section of *Princess Mary* which follows the duel seems to fulfil much the same sequential function with respect to *Princess Mary* except that it is not accorded autonomous structural status. Even so it is strongly marked as a discrete textual entity. The diary form has collapsed, ending the night before the duel. That part of the diary is now regarded as a separate textual entity with which Pechorin finds it difficult to identify: 'It's funny to read over the last page. I thought I might die' (158). The events in Piatigorsk which hitherto formed a predominantly present/future Gestalt while the diary was in dated form, are now regarded as 'the past': 'How clearly and distinctly I remember the past. Time hasn't erased a single line or tint from my memories' (158). This epilogic section of *Princess Mary* also has impressive formal integrity as a text. Even read out of context it would be at once clear from it that two men have been duelling over a woman who has come to hate the surviving duellist. It is further marked as a separate entity by its change of location which, as much as the duel itself, signifies the total closure of the Piatigorsk topos on which the diary was based. It has, in the final paragraph of the story, an epilogue appropriate to the new narrative form, but not to the previous diary structure. If indeed, as my argument is suggesting, the part of *Princess Mary* written at the fort is that story's own '*Maxim Maximych*' it is interesting to consider what such a double reading can tell us about both works. In this discursive concluding part of *Princess Mary* a death (Grushnitsky's) is recollected in detail by Pechorin during Maxim Maximych's absence on a hunting expedition. In *Maxim Maximych* recollection of a death (Bela's) is resisted or refused by

Pechorin ('Pechorin went a shade paler and turned away' [70]) and Maxim is very much present. A valedictory mood is evident in both. In the concluding part of *Princess Mary*, however, Pechorin definitively takes his leave of all the major characters of *Princess Mary*, first Grushnitsky whom he kills, then Vera, then his horse (!), then Werner, and finally Mary.[5] This at once stresses the compact sociality which has dominated the spa setting but also lays starkly bare the utter isolation of Pechorin. In *Maxim Maximych*, by contrast, only one person, Maxim Maximych, is parted with, but he, in his ethnic complexity and ambiguity, also represents the whole of the military/ethnic Caucasian topos which Pechorin has left behind him forever.

Bela and *Princess Mary* represent the extremes of Pechorin's experience in socio-ethnic terms and perhaps in more general European terms. They encapsulate the extremes of civilisation and primitiveness although significantly this extremity is not marked by geographical separation: their propinquity underlines the complexity of the Caucasian situation, its centrality as a defining theme in Russian cultural history and its crucial importance for an understanding of this novel. In both stories Pechorin is a stranger, a Circassian in the spa town, a Petersburg dandy in the frontier fort. Comparison of the two stories reveals remarkable anthropological parallels between the two societies in terms of common human preoccupations, common social conventions and common human impulses.

3. Inter-textual Affinities

Reading *Princess Mary* against other works of Russian literature began with Belinsky, and was undoubtedly the major way in which *A Hero of Our Time* as a whole managed to induct itself into the classical Russian canon. Moreover our manner of approaching character and characterisation in *Princess Mary*, at least in the more conventional literary critical sense, has been fixed in large measure against readings of other works. The text against which *Princess Mary* has been most commonly read is *Eugene Onegin* and inevitably this comparative approach, like most, stresses either the direct influence of the earlier work or the Bloomian dissent which *Princess Mary* introduces. Eikhenbaum, for instance, notes that *Princess Mary* plays with the love plot between Onegin and Tatyana, which is based not on the formula 'I love you' but 'I don't love you' (Eikhenbaum, 1981: 170). In *Eugene Onegin* however this concept is introduced reactively as the hero's response to the heroine's advances. In *Princess Mary* it is developed by Pechorin as a paradoxical way of winning Mary's love, that is used pro-actively and with a kind of dialectical force: from initial hate to ultimate love. As it turns out, however, Pechorin cannot bring himself to feel anything for Mary, unlike the tardy Eugene for Tatyana, and so the full course of the dialectic from Mary's point of view is hate >love > hate, which, it seems, is what Pechorin has wanted all along (since he thanks Princess Mary when she says she hates him!). Gilroy suggests that Mary's reading of romantic novels, like Tatyana's, may have made her susceptible to Pechorin (Gilroy, 1989: 59) seeing herself in the role of his saviour, but there is little active evidence for this in *Princess Mary* and, as Todd points out, literature does not play the same vital characterisational role in *A Hero of Our Time* as it does in *Eugene Onegin* (Todd, 1986: 145).

There are also a number of permutations of character equivalence between Pushkin's and Lermontov's works. The most obvious equation for the male protagonists is that which parallels Pechorin with Onegin and Grushnitsky with Lensky (see Gifford, 1950: 126). However Pechorin may also be regarded as a combination of qualities found in both Onegin and Lensky (he has the latter's artistic talents [Gorelov, 1964: 99]) and Grushnitsky parodies the Lenskian dimension of Pechorin. It would seem symmetrical to equate Olga with Princess Mary and Tatyana with Vera, but Princess Mary's sweet nature and principal role in the story make such an equation, based on the relative age and emotional intensity of the characters, difficult to defend. Gifford sees Princess Mary as combining aspects both of Olga and Tatyana: she has the social graces and good looks of the former but the inner depth of the latter whose fate she broadly shares (Gifford,1950: 126). On the other hand Gorelov has Vera and Princess Mary dividing between them aspects of the single character of Tatyana and there is no doubt that the married Vera does have affinities with the later married Tatyana (Gorelov, 1964: 86). On the other hand Miller finds an unbridgeable gulf separating Vera and Tatyana in terms of the ideals which they incarnate, for whereas Tatyana embodies duty, Vera embodies submission, and these are two incompatible life attitudes (Miller, 1994: 66). The name Vera, however, suggests faith rather than submission, while Mary might be thought to suggest virginal purity. The onomastic symbolism of female names in the novel as a whole does indeed bear out the possibility of some kind of gyno-symbolic system, the four women's names suggesting four manifestations of the feminine principle: faith (Vera); purity (Mary); beauty (Bela); seduction (Ondine). Apart from this, however, we can clearly establish the contours of a character quaternity familiar from *Eugene Onegin* in the persons of Pechorin, Grushnitsky, Princess Mary and Vera. The most obvious way to read these against *Eugene Onegin* would indeed be to conclude that in *Princess Mary* the younger man (Grushnitsky) has now become the shallow fop and the older man has taken on the role of the thinking artist. The older hero now goes for the younger girl, while the Tatyana figure (Vera) complicates the situation by bringing her marriage with her into an early stage of the narrative (rather than at the end as in *Eugene Onegin*).

The characterology of the story reveals very clearly that it is struggling with the legacy of Pushkin's classic and in this it stands at the head of a long line of Russian novels. Its aspiration to novel status as well as its ability to engage intertextually with the seminal work of nineteenth century Russian literature mark *Princess Mary* out as undoubtedly the most important component of *A Hero of Our Time*. It is true that the unique power and impact of Pechorin is generated by all the structural components of *A Hero of Our Time* working in concert. It is unlikely, however, that the novel would have been able to achieve this for its hero if it did not have a society tale such as *Princess Mary* as its core component, capable of engaging at numerous levels with the mainstream of the Russian novelistic tradition.

Notes

1. Both Fokht and Grigoryan were participants in a long and aesthetically fascinating debate during the Soviet period (1960s) on the nature and extent of Romanticism in Russian literature during the nineteenth century. This debate was far from politically irrelevant since Romanticism had been declared a suspect aesthetic during the 1930s because of its ideological affinities with idealism and its consequent opposition to the materialist position underlying the Marxist philosophy of the Communist State.

2. On this see Waszink (1990: 320).

3. On the ambiguity of Pechorin's representing himself as both the actor and the author of other people's tragedies in *Princess Mary* see Rosenshield, (1988: 89-90).

4. On this see the present author's *Pushkins's 'Mozart and Salieri': Themes, Character, Sociology* (Rodopi: Amsterdam, 1995) pp.74 ff.

5. See Gregg (1984: 387-98) for a detailed study of Pechorin's leave-taking.

The Fatalist

1. The Key to the Novel?

As Turner's detailed and useful analysis of *The Fatalist* shows, the work has had an interesting receptive history. Belinsky, in 1841, began a tradition of ignoring its significance by claiming that it did not add anything new to our understanding of Pechorin (Belinsky, 1954: 199). Soviet critics generally put the discussion of fate in the story into a concrete historical context, that of the repressive post-Decembrist regime in which the novel was conceived and written: fatalism was a metaphor for a more general political and philosophical 'reconciliation with reality' (in Hegel's phrase), that is with the reality and inequities of a repressive political regime (Turner, 1978: 56). Under these circumstances Pechorin's apparent resolution in the story not to accept 'fate' (actually he merely agrees with himself to remain sceptical about it) is a progressive encodement of resistance to the regime, albeit passive. Such an approach to the story does however valorise its function beyond what Belinsky had intended and, shorn of its political overtones, forms the basis for more recent, particularly Anglo-American appraisals of the story. Most influential in this regard has been Mersereau's article on the work, subsequently developed in his books (Mersereau, 1960: 137-146).

Mersereau argues that Pechorin rejects fatalism in favour of free will, but, having done so, refuses to take responsibility for his actions. According to such a view *The Fatalist* is the key to the whole of Pechorin's behaviour in the novel since it is in this story that we see Pechorin pondering most deeply about the alternatives of fate and free will. Much significant discussion of the story has centred upon supporting, explicating or refuting Mersereau's opinion. Turner suggests that there is no proper discussion of fate in the story and that the views on fatalism expressed in it are muddled (Turner, 1978: 58). More importantly he cites the novel's creative history, particularly the fact that *The Fatalist* was moved to the end of the novel seemingly as an after-thought before publication, as evidence that it was not meant to serve as a philosophical conclusion to the novel any more than as a formal conclusion (1978: 62). However it has to be said that in a work so formally unorthodox as *A Hero of Our Time* the structural location of components is not a trustworthy indicator of significance either in a positive or a negative sense: the novel does, after all, have an introduction in the middle![1]

Other commentators have taken a more compromising view about Pechorin's attitude to fate. Herbert Eagle suggests that Pechorin treats fate as he treats other abstract concepts likely to affect his activity, as a kind of pragmatic myth, a supposition or basis on which he acts while doubting it at the same time (Eagle, 1994: 312). Garrard thinks that Pechorin is convinced that fate governs existence, although his concept of it weights the scales in favour of free will (Garrard, 1982: 143). He sees this particular attitude as an anticipation of Ivan Karamazov's views on the nature of good and evil (138). In general, however, it seems to the present writer that the question of *The Fatalist*'s 'role' in the novel as a whole, if it is not (as I think obvious) simply a crude matter of terminal position, is better investigated structurally than thematically, that is in relation to its structural orientation to the other component stories in the novel. A thematic investigation must inevitably centre on the abstractions of fate and free will, the very definition of which is open to considerable subjective variation as the heterodox views listed above demonstrate. For this reason it seems convenient to begin our consideration of *The Fatalist* with a discussion of its heterotelic function, that is its affinities and contrasts, on the widest possible number of levels, with the other constituent stories of the novel.

2. Heterotelic Features

The search for structural affinities between *The Fatalist* and other stories quickly reveals a fact which may underlie the long debate about its problematic status and semantic sterility. Its setting, theme, plot and characterisation are such as to prevent it having obviously close affinities with any of the other component works of the novel. Neither can we easily twin it with any other of the stories singly as can be done quite impressively in the case of *Taman* and *Bela*. We can indeed make quite a striking list of things which it does not have in common with the other stories either individually or collectively. It does not, for instance, have the framing device of arrival, enforced stay, and departure which is common to *Taman* and *Maxim Maximych*. It does not have the central sexual theme of abduction/seduction which is common to *Bela, Taman* and *Princess Mary*. It does not have the theme of sorrowful departure found in all the other stories except *Bela* (it ends indeed with Pechorin's *arrival* back at the fort). It is an all-male story like *Maxim Maximych* but it is hard to find any common androcentric theme. There is much therefore in what the other stories do and how they are told, which is avoided or denied in *The Fatalist*. This, however, since it is negative information, tells us little other than to confirm the work's relative isolation in what is otherwise a tissue of intertextual correspondences.

There are still, however, some significant parallels and contrasts. These involve mainly the degree of Pechorin's involvement with others, both in the sense of intimacy, or lack of it, and in the dynamic sense of interaction with them to produce change. Regarding the latter form of involvement we can trace

in very broad terms a kind of threefold grammar of social interaction, according
to the pattern recently set out by André Van Holk with reference to *Princess
Mary* (Van Holk: 1992). Pechorin's interactions in a given milieu proceed
according to a threefold model of 1) observation; 2) interference; 3) victimisa-
tion. In *Taman* Pechorin is first observer, then interferer, then victim. In *Maxim
Maximych* the Narrator is observer, interferer (because he insists out of curiosity
– the mainspring of interference – on finding out who owns the smart carriage
which has arrived) and Maxim is victim; (the Narrator is an exceptional
beneficiary because he gains something – the notes – from the encounter). In
Bela Pechorin is observer, interferer and victimiser. In *Princess Mary* Pechorin
is much the same only on a more heightened and calculated level. In *Princess
Mary* and *Bela*, unlike *The Fatalist* and *Taman*, the hero is not standing alone
but is positively abetted by a character cast in the role of confidant (Maxim
Maximych; Werner). In *The Fatalist*, as in *Taman*, there is no such person to
play this role but, whereas in *Taman* the social 'collective' confronting Pechorin
is hostile (he is an outsider trying to get closer to the smugglers, to know, to
solve) in *The Fatalist* Pechorin is among people like himself, officers who are
neither close enough to be classed as friends nor sufficiently alienated to be
deemed hostile or inimical.

In fact, it is at first Vulich who stands out as isolated. Between the story's
opening and the moment when Pechorin makes his bet, the narrative voice
is in effect a collective one, a spokesman for the undifferentiated *vse* ('all')
of the group, and, if first person at all, then plural, rather than singular. The
process is therefore the reverse of that in *Taman*, the hero beginning from a
position of relative social integration and moving towards greater individu-
ation through his interaction with Vulich, so that, by the end of the evening,
all were 'probably...agreeing that I'd been selfish to bet against a man who
was going to shoot himself' (179). However Pechorin would not have been
induced to put himself in this isolated position were it not that Vulich
himself, already marked out from the crowd by his eccentricity, had on this
occasion decided to 'test fate'. Although Pechorin frankly admits later in the story
that his own test of fate was 'like' that of Vulich, the imitation of Vulich on
Pechorin's part begins much earlier, with his challenging him to a bet.

That Pechorin may in effect be pretending to emulate Vulich, and is thus
drawn into participation in the proceedings at an early stage, does have
important resonances elsewhere in the novel. In *Princess Mary* it is Grushnitsky's prior admiration of the heroine that gives Pechorin the idea of becoming
involved and supplanting him, and this competitive attitude is reinforced by a
formalised rhetoric of emulation: '*Mon cher, je haïs les hommes pour ne pas les
mépriser, car autrement la vie serait une farce trop dégoutante*'; '*Mon cher...je
méprise les femmes pour ne pas les aimer, car autrement la vie serait une
mélodrame trop ridicule*' (96-7); and, at an early stage in the association between
Werner and Pechorin: 'I'm convinced...that one fine day, sooner or later, I shall

die'; 'I'm convinced...that one foul evening I had the misfortune to be born' (p.101). The same tendency can be detected in *Bela* too: Azamat effectively says to Kazbich 'I'll steal my sister for you if you give me your horse' (p.33); Pechorin effectively says to Azamat 'I'll steal Kazbich's horse for you if you will steal your sister for me' (p.35). *The Fatalist* presents the same kind of competitive process as if it were a bout of vying at cards and this may provide a ludic key to the persistent motif: 1) Vulich: 'I suggest we try it out on ourselves'(177); 2) Other players (passing the bid): 'Not me!'; 3) 'What about a bet?' says Pechorin, raising the ante; 4) 'What on?' asks Vulich, seeing Pechorin; 5) '...there's no such thing as predestination' says Pechorin, in effect raising again with twenty gold coins; 6) 'Taken!' says Vulich seeing the raise. Once Vulich has taken up the bet the matter must go to a show of cards, i.e. Vulich must prove whether there is predestination or not – more specifically whether he *has* predestination or not.

If anything, then, *The Fatalist* does not engage with the other stories on the matter of fate, since most critics agree either that it is not discussing fate at all, or does not discuss it properly. It does however sum up the nature of Pechorin's engagement with those he comes into contact with in the course of the novel, revealing the importance of other people's ideas in providing the progressive stimuli for Pechorin's actions. Along with *Bela* and *Princess Mary* it illustrates that Pechorin's gift is one of sublime imitation, which, beginning with attraction to another's ideas or actions, transcends these dialectically in order to attain a perfection and originality beyond the reach of the original object of emulation. In this process, those who have supplied the original idea, inspiration or behavioral pattern, get no credit for them, once they have been eclipsed by Pechorin, who, like the wren in the fable, outflies the eagle by hiding in its feathers. Appropriation and improvement by Pechorin is inseparable from the disappropriation and disempowerment of others. It may be that one of *The Fatalist*'s functions is to lay bare this characteristic of Pechorin, but this function is not related to the work's terminal position; indeed, its explicatory force in relation to the other stories is largely a matter of contrast, and we may equally claim that it is *Princess Mary* which lays bare the full social implications of this vying process while in *The Fatalist*, these are obscured by a spurious experiment with fate.

We may reach other general conclusions about the relation of *The Fatalist* to the novel as a whole. It is clearly connected to it in terms of overall plot by the appearance of Maxim Maximych at the conclusion. One commentator suggests, not too extravagantly, that there are two fatalists in the story, Vulich and Maxim Maximych (Dynnik, 1982: 151), and it is striking that Maxim, after exerting himself to find a mechanistic explanation for Vulich's experiment, in terms of his experience of guns in the Caucasus, adds, almost as a reflex, that literally, 'It must have been written for him from birth' to die at the hands of the Cossack. It is perhaps significant that the Foote

translation considerably tones down the fatalistic implications of this statement: 'I suppose that's how he was *meant* to die' (184 [my italics]) – without
strictly mistranslating it, possibly because it may have seemed in its literal
form inconsistent with a 'commonsensical' reading of Maxim's character.
In fact, if Maxim Maximych really is a fatalist, many of his apparently
contradictory attitudes and actions highlighted earlier in this study become
clearer. His acquiescence, for instance, to Pechorin's activities with Bela,
and his generally Hamletic unwillingness to take firm action or reprisals for
any of the misdemeanours committed in *Bela* are certainly more understand-
able if he is seen to have, or to have acquired, a fatalistic attitude to life.

Lotman's discussion of fate in *The Fatalist* clearly connects it to the presence
of an oriental dimension within it and the novel as a whole. He regards Lermontov
as deeply concerned about Russian national identity and the relationship
within it of occidental and oriental elements (Lotman,1985: 16). In *The Fatalist*
this preoccupation becomes individuated in terms of personal psychology.
Critics have traditionally held that Vulich, as a Serb, is meant to represent the
east and eastern ideas, but there is no need to import orientalism into this story
(or indeed into the novel as a whole), since it is set in a Cossack settlement on
the edge of the muslim east, while Pechorin himself is on leave from a Russian
fort in muslim Chechnya. Moreover, as Lotman makes clear, the two dominant
metaphysical views, western voluntarism and eastern fatalism, struggle for
supremacy in Pechorin's mind, his sceptical western side judging his fatalistic
eastern (Lotman, 1985: 15). When Pechorin decides to attack the Cossack, says
Lotman, this is the western counterpart of the 'eastern' act which Vulich carries
out on himself (1985: 15) for Vulich already believes in fate when he fires the
gun, whereas Pechorin is making a calculated act having first weighed up the
odds. If Lotman's picture of a divided Pechorin, part east, part west, is accepted,
it also implies a Maxim Maximych far closer to the east, far more aculturated,
indeed, than most criticism has hitherto suggested.

3.   A Game of Chance

After having assessed the nature and degree of the inter-relationship between
The Fatalist and the other stories in *A Hero of Our Time* we now move to a
more detailed consideration of the story in terms of its philosophical theme
and the way it is unfolded. Given that the majority of commentators insist
that it does not deal with the subject of fate very well, if at all, we can
legitimately begin our discussion by asking what therefore *The Fatalist* is
about. Firstly, as Turner has noted, it is not fate proper which is discussed
in the story, but one particular aspect which he calls the *terminus vitae*
(Turner, 1978: 57). However it seems not surprising that this aspect of fate
should be the one discussed in the story, given its context. The cast of *The
Fatalist* are officers who have been involved in hand-to-hand fighting with
muslim Chechens. They are likely to have had a keen personal interest in the

time of their death and also in a belief widely held by those they were fighting, who, like the ancient astrologists conjured up by Pechorin later in the story, derived their strength from a belief in this particular form of predestination.

It is also the case that the story develops out of a discussion about fate which has reached an inconclusive stage. In this sense *The Fatalist* should be read as a story about certain attitudes about fate and certainly not be dismissed if these attitudes are flawed or philosophically ineffective: the story seems to have been persistently misread as though *it should have* produced proper conclusions about fate, whereas we are warned by the major at the outset that all discussion may be flawed by lack of an adequate empirical method: '"All this proves nothing, gentlemen," said the old major. "You quote all these odd incidents to back up your views, but none of you actually saw them happen."' (175).

The major highlights a fact which has already been mentioned by Pechorin as narrator, that the view under discussion is essentially a belief and not a philosophy, and, as a belief, is more likely to be promoted in discussion by exemplification rather than proof. Again, the long reflective passage which represents Pechorin's thoughts after leaving his fellow officers underlines the fact that it was the ancients' belief in the efficacy of celestial influence which gave them inner strength and not the fact of that influence, which a modern like himself does not accept. Furthermore, the belief under discussion is not merely pre-destination but *pre-scription*, the metaphor, in other words, for the pre-ordination of a person's death, as having been written in advance, as though in a book. A metaphorical text can never be scrutinised; its contents remain unknown and its veracity untestable: 'Where are the reliable witnesses who have seen the list with the hour of our death on it?' (175). The textual metaphor is appropriate to the case because in any form of textualised narrative (or in film for that matter) action is fixed and unchangeable. Uncertainties and multiple possibilities encountered in the reading process are merely symptoms of the reader's temporary lack of knowledge, for in fact there are no contingencies, and only that which has already been written will come to pass in the narrative. Clearly, then, among theories of pre-destination that which uses the scriptive metaphor has a natural affinity to narrative fiction and the relevance of this scriptive fate to *A Hero of Our Time* should be apparent to us from discussions earlier in this study, particularly those relating to *Princess Mary*. Since a fictionalised figure is fated by its fiction, is emplotment or dramatisation a way of 'fating' life, of ensuring its predictability on a wider level? Are human beings themselves 'scripted'? *The Fatalist* explicitly addresses these problems which have already exercised Pechorin in the two previous stories, but offers no solution. However, although these matters clearly do resonate with concerns elsewhere in the novel this may not be the principal reason for their inclusion in *The Fatalist*. Indeed it is precisely the non-provability of all the matters and incidents relating to fate in the story which drive it on and constitute its interest.

The inconclusiveness of both the discussion of and experiment on fate conducted in the story leaves us free to investigate the possibility of other thematic dominants or co-dominants in the story. For instance, it could be claimed with some justification that the story is not so much about fate, as about gambling. Vulich is established in the story as an inveterate gambler; his test with the gun is a gamble in response to a bet, and Pechorin's attack on the Cossack is also a gamble in the sense of a calculated risk. We noted above that Pechorin's exchange with Vulich took the form of a vye. However this vying does not automatically follow from the fact that Vulich is a gambler since gambling takes many forms. We are therefore furnished with an incident by which to judge Vulich's expertise in this regard. Vulich is engaged as banker in a game of chance at the moment of a Circassian attack. Superficially the whole incident seems to prefigure the later event at the major's quarters. There is betting, followed by a context in which Vulich runs a strong risk of being shot. The incident demonstrates the extreme bravery of Vulich (he 'didn't bother about the bullets and swords' and 'charged forward at the head of some soldiers' [176]) but also his extreme addiction to gambling ('Vulich didn't move..."Stake the bank", he called' [176]). This contextual information is necessary to motivate Vulich's offer to 'try it out on ourselves' (177): he is just the man to take such a risk, for the two dominants in his characterisation thus far are bravery and gambling.

The story itself opens in the aftermath of card play. Vulich, as we have seen, is characterised by card play and Pechorin will signal the moment for Vulich to fire by dropping a card. However, although in each case a pack of fifty-two is used, the games are several. That which the officers abandon for their discussion is a social game related to whist. The game played on Vulich's pillow during the Circassian attack is an unspecified banking game clearly akin to those, like faro or lansquenet, in which the gambling element depends entirely on the chance turn of a card. The card dropped by Pechorin as his signal to Vulich has ceased to be a card in the true sense; whereas it must have mattered to the officer playing with Vulich during the attack that it was the seven, and not any other card, which turned up, in this case the denomination of the card is unimportant: 'I think it was the ace of hearts' (but another card would have served just as well for Pechorin's signal [178]).

Although this would seem radically to differentiate what transpires from any recognisable game of cards, Vulich does in fact make it clear that it is not merely different, but better – 'This is better than faro or banker' (179) – to which Pechorin replies 'rather more dangerous though' (179). It may be, from what we know of Vulich, that its betterness resides precisely in the fact that it is dangerous. On the other hand it may be that Vulich is here referring to the fact that he has emerged the winner. We are told, for instance, that he usually lost, but that on the night of the Circassian attack he was 'having a terrific run of luck' (176). This again runs counter to what he tells Pechorin when the latter informs him that he has 'gambler's luck' namely that it is for the first time in his life. All this obliges us to put a particular gloss on the unusual gambling incident. Vulich's luck changed when the punter staked his successful seven; he has cleared Vulich out, hence the disagreeableness of the task of taking him his winnings, which duty, however, Vulich so promptly carries out. A similar diligence about settling losses is evident in Vulich's question to the assembled officers as to which of them 'will pay my twenty gold pieces' (177) i.e. settle up with Pechorin if he is killed. Concern over this matter suggests Vulich's uncertainty about his own survival, but this would not necessarily conflict with his belief in predestination, for believing is one thing and knowing the time and place is another. From this point of view, therefore, a negative outcome to Vulich's experiment would not disprove predestination: it would simply show that, if pre-destination exists, Vulich is predestined to die *now*. The point about Vulich, however, is that he is a gambler, recklessly brave, and a loser. Thus, he is just the person to want to gamble on such a risky business...and to lose. Pechorin has clearly guessed the latter likelihood. It is precisely the losing which characterises the nature of Vulich's gambling: gambling must be his all-consuming passion if 'his lack of success only made him more persistent' (176).

Pechorin's offer of a bet sets the whole project in motion, for until this moment, Vulich, speaking as wreckless man, rather than gambler, has had a universally negative response to 'trying it out on ourselves'. The element of vying in Pechorin's manner of accomplishing his end has already been touched upon. Importantly, this mode of betting is suggestive of a quite different form of card game than that which Vulich is used to, for, in such games, those of the poker variety, though betting is involved, the success of the outcome depends less upon luck than upon the ability of a player to persuade his opponent to fold or show his hand when it would have been better for him not to have done so. Pechorin, like a cunning poker player, uses what he knows of his opponent's weaknesses to lure him into bidding. Having got Vulich to agree to bid he stakes high ('all that I had in my pocket'[177]). Vulich accepts the bid 'with a hollow voice' and has to borrow from the Major to complete the large stake. This is a game with no clear rules. What, for instance, if Vulich's will fails him? Does he lose his stake? The answer is probably yes. A man who would carry money across a battle-field to pay someone he has just lost to at cards has a keen sense of honour. It is in Pechorin's interest to make him fold. If he is killed (and he is sure to be killed) a mighty argument will ensue over whether Pechorin can claim his winnings, since, whatever else the experiment achieves, Vulich's death will not prove that there is no predestination.

Sitting at the table, Pechorin tries to unnerve his opponent, as a good poker player should, and stares at him intently. He tells him (lying) that he is certain to lose his life. Vulich, however, remains unmoved. Subsequent bets are made, though not by Pechorin, on whether the pistols are loaded. These, of course, are totally unrelated to the original, since the answer to this question can be ascertained without firing a shot. They underline, however, that the performance now in progress has definitively passed from the philosophical into the ludic. Indeed, it has translated itself almost effortlessly from the code of one of the circumscribed preoccupations of the military – the possibility of death – into another: gambling. Since gambling is his obsession Vulich appears to have triumphed in effecting this transformation into his favourite code which he has now aggrandised beyond all precedent. He is empowered: 'he had acquired some mysterious power over us' (177), yet Pechorin's role in Vulich's acquisition of this power is as subtle as it is crucial.

The ballistic games played in this small military circle are not new to Pechorin. He has played something similar with Grushnitsky. In that game he had not only information about his opponent's character but also about the guns. The very point which is not known in *The Fatalist* and makes the game worthwhile is, in *Princess Mary*, known to perfection by the opponent. In *Princess Mary* Pechorin has effectively seen Grushnitsky's hand and so can bid with assurance. Grushnitsky has said six paces; Pechorin sees six paces and raises – six paces along the side of a cliff. Grushnitsky is agitated but agrees. Pechorin looks hard at Grushnitsky after he has won the toss. Grushnitsky trembles but aims his gun. Pechorin is angry but says nothing. Grushnitsky lowers his gun: 'I can't do it' (165). In fact Grushnitsky does shoot at Pechorin in the end and only grazes him – deliberately. What is effectively the second part of the duel, that is Pechorin's turn to shoot, is the antithesis of *The Fatalist* incident. As in that story 'Pechorin stared him hard in the face to see if there were any signs of remorse' (165-6). He sees no sign. He assures Grushnitsky that he is going to die, but, of course, Pechorin's gun is at this moment not loaded. In this case the precise state of the gun's priming is known to both players; even so, there is still room for error, since Grushnitsky does not know that Pechorin knows that the gun is not loaded.

In *Princess Mary* therefore epistemic suspense about the state of the gun revolves around the moral issues of trickery and deceit, whereas in *The Fatalist* it concerns the ulimate existential issue of life or death. Even so, in both cases Pechorin seeks to play as much as possible on the weaknesses of his respective opponents in the different contexts. Moral scruple is the weakness which nearly makes Grushnitsky fold; fear of losing nearly has the same effect on Vulich. These similarities should not be surprising. It is difficult to define the precise cultural status of duelling, whether as ritual or as conflict or as punishment. It seems, however, to have many affinities with game, and rightly so, since in some of its manifestations, formalised sword play, for instance, it clearly does cross the boundary into sport. Duelling, gambling, hunting, sword-play and skirmishing: these martial rituals are important elements in *A Hero of Our Time*, and help to establish a core context of military culture in the novel.[2]

4.   Philosophy and Rhetoric

Although, as this study has attempted to show so far, discussion of fate in *The Fatalist* is effectively usurped by play, this does not mean that there are no philosophical implications in what takes place. Luck in card games (here I somewhat adapt a view of Lotman's: 1985: 13) may be considered by players either as fate or chance depending on their point of view, but it is one and the same hidden process of causality which produces the turned-up card however its appearance is explained. In the same way winning and losing are essentially different perspectives on the same phenomenon. Concepts such as good or bad luck are really, in Bacon's terms, *idola specus*, delusions arising from imperfect knowledge, since, although, say, cards move according to rational mechanical laws during shuffling, card play deliberately prevents participants seeing these laws in operation. Thus the intense argument which broke out among the officers as to why Vulich's gun did not fire, and which is taken up at the end of *The Fatalist* by Maxim Maximych, is perfectly legitimate. Some mechanical process, or failure of mechanical process, must have prevented the gun from firing the first time and enabled it to fire the second time, however unusual or unlikely such a process might be. It is also the case that the terms luck and fate are interchangeable in most contexts involving chance, because they are interchangeable synonyms for the unpredictability of events. Fate, however, is more commonly used of chance events which radically affect an individual's life than in arbitrary rituals like gaming which exploit chance in a less existentially crucial way. However, in Vulich's case, the two states combine: his gambling becomes an obsession which rules his life; his lack of expertise at it becomes a fatal quality. His willingness to risk his life is a play with his fate, not just with luck, because it involves life itself. These considerations tend to suggest that what is being investigated in *The Fatalist* is a kind of mixture of fate and chance, a rather eerie hybrid which the unusual inner constitution of Vulich gives birth to, for which the Greek term *tyche* seems to be most appropriate.

Two complicating factors enter Vulich's test. First is the fact that the gun did fire on a second attempt. This successful discharge clearly has to be regarded as part of the overall event which establishes the likelihood of predestination. If Vulich had been predestined to die at the moment he pulled the trigger, the gun would have gone off. But, clearly, if there is no predestination, the gun could also still have gone off. If there *is* predestination and the gun had not gone off, then Vulich was predestined not to die *at that moment* but, equally, if there is no predestination Vulich could still have pulled the trigger and not died. Although this complex of possibilities has led critics to suggest that Vulich's test is therefore pointless, this need not be so. As we suggested above, since predestination cannot be proved, and is therefore a belief, acceptance (or rejection) of it is likely to be the result of persuasion rather than proof, of rhetoric rather than logic. As the narrating voice says at the opening of the story: 'Everyone had some strange story to tell for and against' (175). Such rhetorical corroborations are in Bacon's terms *idola fori* - popular beliefs – rather than *idola specus* - speculations about luck and chance based on restricted information.

An important rhetorical factor is the ballistic state of the gun. This is not known at first, the major, by whose bed it hung, being 'so perplexed that he couldn't rightly remember' (178). One of the company, however, weights the argument in favour of its being loaded: 'Come off it...It was hanging by the bed, so it's bound to be loaded' (178). Nevertheless the test starts in some uncertainty about the state of the gun which Vulich does not seek to dispel because he is not trying to execute himself but to allow fate (or chance) to determine the outcome. In fact, however, the gun was loaded and it is precisely this information which is not available to Vulich or any of his witnesses. If it were, however, and had Vulich gone ahead with the test, the outcome would still have been the same but there would then have been no need for Vulich to fire a second time to prove that the gun was loaded all along. Yet this, too, will not do. Though loaded, and, in our hypothetical case, known by all to be loaded, the gun misfired. This is rhetorically very powerful in favour of predestination and yet still not potent enough. A misfire is a recognised technical term in ordnance. To the non-believer, even knowing that the gun was loaded, a misfire would be simply a mechanical fluke. For this reason, irrespective of whether the status of the gun before firing were known precisely or not, the really crucial rhetorical device is the second shot; this it is which seems to argue that the bullet refused to strike Vulich specifically, since, as soon as the gun was pointed away from him it reverted to its normal behaviour and fired. Vulich's ability to convince depends on the gun's firing successfully a second time, though not at him of course!

This second shot establishes a pattern of persuasion which persists through all the significant events of the story. Predestined events are not manifested in themselves, but always *post factum* in the light of some other event. Thus, for the true believer (and Pechorin is briefly a believer) although the first shot fulfilled the predestined act (saved Vulich from death, that is) the second event (the shot from which Vulich was saved) is the one which persuades. And this is because binarity characterises the language of persuasion: not *this*, but *that*; *this* rather than *that*; maybe *this* but certainly *that*; since it compares and evaluates (which singularity cannot do) but does not argue, unlike the complexity of the syllogism.

The rhetoric of binarity extends beyond predestination to the sub-theme of prescience which Pechorin, rather than Vulich, introduces into the story. The structural binarity of prescience ensures that the episode with the gun will have a sequel beyond Vulich's immediate survival. 'I fancied I saw the mark of death on his pale face' (177). Whereas predestination was the common conversational concern of the gathered officers, prescience concerns only Pechorin and Vulich. Yet Pechorin's prescience is the same kind of *idolum fori* as predestination. Although only Pechorin seems to have noticed the mark of death on Vulich, he supports his belief by the fact that 'A lot of old soldiers say the same...' (177-8). Also, while we may be willing to accept that Pechorin has noticed such a thing for himself, we may doubt his claim that he has always noticed it in circumstances of imminent death, or that it has always been there to be noticed, for we hear nothing of this phenomenon in *Princess Mary* where Pechorin had ample opportunity to scrutinise Grushnitsky's face for such symptoms. As we have seen, Pechorin's remark to Vulich (which concerns not the mark of death, the *signum*, but its *signatum*, the fact that Vulich will die) – 'You're going to die today' – belongs to the quite separate rhetoric of betting and vying. After Vulich has survived, Pechorin raises the subject again not in relation to the signifier but to the signified: '...I can't understand why I was so sure you were going to die today' (179). However, in terms of the *signum* this statement has two formulations: either 'what I saw was not the mark of death' or 'the mark I saw is not always of death'. This misreading has some affinities with Pechorin's misreading of the blind boy in *Taman*, but unlike it, it is only temporarily wrong, for Vulich will indeed die that day.

The mark of death is, of course, an instrument of prescience as a sign is an instrument of cognition. From its temporal orientation it should undoubtedly be classed as an omen, that is a token of some future event to which it is not causally related (the involvement of causality producing symptoms or prognostications rather than omens). However, it is precisely contamination by the symptomatic which makes the 'mark of death' a problematic omen. There is clearly a possibility that the strain and fear of facing death may alter features, and that, if this happens, it may affect some, like Vulich, who face death but do not actually die. However even if the mark of death is an omen in the genuine sense and indicates only those who will die, it is, like all omens, only confirmable by the event it presages. Moreover, omens, like all signs, may also exist in non-signifying forms (my black cat is not an omen for me) and will be relegated to these forms if they fail to function as an omen. Thus an omen is identified as such *post factum* (the black cat *was* an omen today because immediately after it *x* occurred). For Pechorin's *sign* to be an *omen* Vulich has to die. Within a fictional narrative, moreover, structural imperatives make it unlikely that an omen introduced under circumstances such as those in *The Fatalist* will not prove itself true; in the literary context, it becomes a device for arousing lectorial expectations which are likely to be satisfied in due course. The fictional text, then, as we suggested above, tends towards the creation of a predestined world and may become part of the rhetorical support for predestination.

Importantly prescience does not imply fatalism. The fact that a person knows that something will happen means, if he truly knows, that it *will* happen, but not that nothing could have been done to prevent its occurrence. Furthermore, if we have a true prescience of someone's death, there is nothing to prevent us trying to prevent it; that is, we will be able to take real preventative measures, although they will be ineffective. In the case of Pechorin, assuming for a moment that the mark of death really was present, and predicted Vulich's death at the hands of the Cossack, Pechorin is prevented from taking action to avert Vulich's death because the intervening episode has made him doubt the veracity of the omen. Only after the event is it recognised by Pechorin for what it is – an omen – by which time it is too late to alter its relation to the event.

True predestination has a logical rather than an epistemological basis. Since Aristotle the argument in its favour has run that, since the occurrence of an event in the past is subject to the simple criteria of truth or falsehood, so events in the future must also be susceptible to these same criteria: of the two statements 'Vulich will be killed'/'Vulich will not be killed' one is now true and one now false and therefore the future is unalterable. Although Vulich does evoke this binary before shooting at himself (literally 'I might, I might not' [178]) this rationally based, essentially western argument for fate does not figure in the thinking of either Pechorin or his fellow officers. Since the 'list' on which predestined names are written is a text it is presumed to be intelligible: if we or our 'witnesses' could study it we would *know* the hour of our doom. In this way the view of fate unfolded here is essentially identical with foreknowledge: there is a *foreknower* who puts us on the list, and if we saw the latter we would also foreknow. Such a view of fate must be essentially occasionalist in conception: if Vulich must die, at a particular hour, all sorts of evasive actions will have to have been taken to prevent him dying earlier. It is precisely such proof which the officers are looking for and think they have found in *The Fatalist*. Such occasionalism also turns the laws of cause and effect upside down since it is now possible for a future event to 'cause' an event in the past, something which would otherwise be logically impossible. For the fact that Vulich must die at the hands of a Cossack, and only in that way, means that he must be prevented from dying earlier, or put more starkly, his future death is the cause of his not dying now. It is true, of course, that viewed in retrospect, after he has died, Vulich's, or any person's, death will be a logical impossibility at any earlier date. But, again, it is retrospection alone which reveals this to us.

In the digression which intervenes between his episode with Vulich and his attack on the Cossack, Pechorin reflects upon the strength to be derived from a belief in predestination, but he also seems to hint at the undesirability of prescience. As a boy he effectively lived his life in advance, in idealised romantic terms, so that, when he came to live it in fact, he 'found it boring and disgusting like reading a poor pastiche of a long familiar book' (180). To script life in advance is to ruin life, whether according to a romantic (as here) or fatalistic template. Better take it as it comes.

Shortly after these musings Pechorin ensures that the plot of *The Fatalist* will remain an essentially masculine one, for he turns down an incipient romance (anticipative of Tolstoy's *The Cossacks*) with his landlord's daughter and thus again emulates Vulich who 'never ran after the Cossack girls...' (176). Vulich himself is struck down by the drunken Cossack in circumstances which have strong rhetorically persuasive properties. Firstly, the murder comes shortly after the curious event witnessed by Pechorin and the officers. Secondly, it has no causal connection with it. Vulich has clearly been spared for a future death and here is that death, one which, though close in time, is quite contingent to the original experiment. The Cossack also behaves like an agent of fate, using, as Barratt and Briggs point out a dependable sword rather than that species of weapon, the reliability of which has so recently has been called into doubt, and singling Vulich out with his 'you!' (Barratt and Briggs, 1989: 111) as though he were a divine messenger. However other circumstances surrounding the killing detract from this effect. The Cossack is drunk; he is, literally, 'attacking all he sees'.[3] This includes a pig as well as Vulich. These two events, the killing of the pig and the killing of Vulich, parody the elegant duplex structure of Vulich's original experiment. However, whereas, in this experiment, the second event defines the first as fatalistically significant (the gun firing on the second try suggesting the possibility of some preordained survival for Vulich) here the first event undermines the second: the murder of Vulich alone would have been more persuasive than the murder of Vulich together with a pig. Vulich's dying words ('He was right') are taken by Pechorin to refer to his own prediction of Vulich's death; they could, however, refer to the Cossack, who, since drunk, might have been thought not to have been looking for Vulich in particular, but, as agent of fate, is indeed looking precisely for him.

The subsequent siege of the Cossack is, in some ways, less remarkable for Pechorin's role in it, which only serves to continue his characteristic emulation of Vulich, than for the reaction of Yefimich and the other Cossacks. The Cossacks' ambiguous ethnic identity serves as a pretext for reintroducing the eastern motif of fate at the level of theory rather than practice. Yefimich is urged to have a conscience and give himself up, conscience being identified with the Christian Slav by the speaker, rather than the Chechen: 'You're an honest Christian, aren't you, not some plaguey Chechen?' (183). At the same time, in giving himself up, the Cossack 'must just face up to it and take what comes' ([183] more literally: 'You can't escape your *fate*' [my italics]). When his mother is asked to intervene she refuses, although a little earlier she had looked 'frantic with despair' and appeared to be uttering 'a whispered prayer or curse' (183). This albeit sparse characterisation is sufficient to suggest that, though concerned, she refuses to act, again suggesting, perhaps, the same resignation to fate as that being urged on her son by the other Cossacks. Pechorin's measured act of daring is framed by these intimations of a widespread fatalism among the Cossack community and the concluding words of Maxim Maximych, already discussed above. Maxim's simple assertion of the principle of predestination and his impatience, according to Pechorin, with metaphysical speculation, create the final impression of an osmotic fatalism, transfusing itself subtly into those who linger in the Caucasus.

Notes

1. Both of these ideas (the arbitrary position of The Fatalist and of the medial introduction) are treated by Eikhenbaum (1961: 282; 1981: 167).

2. Among others Hingley (1964: 206-7) and Richards (1985: 23) have pointed out the military dimension in Lermontov's novel, Richards in particular stressing the martial traits of Pechorin.

3. This is the literal translation of the Russian; Foote's translation (p.81) is considerably freer.

By Way of a Conclusion

'...the first and also the last thing in a book...(19)'

The Introductions: 'Author's Preface' and Foreword to Pechorin's Journal

Surprisingly little critical attention has been devoted to what I will generically term 'The Introductions': the author's preface to the second edition of the novel (hereafter the 'Preface') and to the foreword to Pechorin's Journal (the 'Foreword'). This is all the more remarkable since a good deal of what is tacitly accepted as being 'about' either Pechorin or the novel as a whole, is coloured by what is contained in them: that Pechorin's Journal is a frank confession, because its writer had no intention to publish, that Pechorin is a kind of collective portrait of his generation, and, most of all, in recent years, that irony is the key to the work. In fact, however, the veridical status of the introductions' discourse is particularly problematical since, while there is a good case for considering both of them as part of the fictional apparatus of the novel, they are so positioned as to require the most potent rhetoric to justify the truth of what they contain. Thus, at the precise point in the Preface where we are told that we, as readers, must learn to understand irony, the ironies and contradictions in the discourse which is telling us this are at their most intense.

Of the two introductions the Preface has the more problematic status. Turner, for instance, in a particularly useful analysis of the discursive problems involved, decides that it should not be regarded as an integral part of the text of *A Hero of Our Time* at all, because it belongs to a Lermontov who stands outside it. Cornwell, while accepting that it has come to be treated as an integral part of the text, concedes that this incorporation is somewhat 'unusual' and 'irregular' (Cornwell, 1995: xvi). Krupyshev (1989: 63-6) though not explicit on the point, appears to treat the Preface as in some way a part of the integral structure. Before approaching the status of the Preface in greater detail, however, it may be useful to review the prevalent critical views on both it and the Foreword.

Unlike the Preface the Foreword has been universally regarded as an integral part of the fiction. Barratt and Briggs see the Narrator as a passive mouthpiece or ventriloquist for Pechorin's ideas and his discourse as aimed at creating uncritical receptivity for Pechorin's ideas (Barratt and Briggs, 1989: 45). However, the voice of the Narrator, particularly in articulating his philanthropic ideas towards the public, seems rather different from Pechorin's. For reasons that are not easy to follow, Barratt and Briggs also claim that the Narrator must be called 'Pechorin'. They do this on the grounds that the Narrator claims in the Foreword to be 'putting my own name to somebody else's work' (75) and that this 'work' refers to the Journal only, since the notes are his own work anyway. Since he has also 'changed all the names' (75) the hero of *Taman*, *Bela* and *The Fatalist* would not have been called Pechorin in the first place. This is a very interesting point of view, but, I think, untenable. 'Putting one's name to' is not exactly the same as 'claiming to have written' and indeed plagiarism, which is clearly what the Narrator is sensitive to here, is rarely in the former category, since the plagiarist is usually trying to pass off extracts from existing works under the guise of his own; the sensitivity of the Narrator, then, is precisely to the fact that, having lost his travel notes, he is having to rely on another's work to provide him with enough material for a book.

Probably the most useful work on the introductions has been done by Turner, less perhaps because of his treatment of the two texts *per se*, but because he sets out an excellent model for the narrative hierarchy in the introductions and in the novel as a whole which I too shall adapt in the discussion which follows. Turner isolates four roles for Lermontov's involvement with the novel. Lermontov 1 is the real Lermontov who breathed, lived and died; Lermontov 2 is the implied author of *A Hero of Our Time* – that is Lermontov the originator of the fictional narrative voices in the novel; Lermontov 3 is the Narrator who gives us *Bela*, *Maxim Maximych* and the *Foreword*; Lermontov 4 is Pechorin. Lermontov 3 and Lermontov 4 are clearly contentious identifications in that, as 'fictional characters' in the way that Lermontov 1 and Lermontov 2 are not, they need not *necessarily* be equated with their author. However, it should be obvious that there is heuristic value in considering them in relation to the author's identity, especially in a context in which Lermontov's public clearly had made an identification between him and these figures.

There is never any question of Lermontov 4 writing either of the introductions. However, as Barratt and Briggs suggest, he may have indirectly influenced the Foreword which is, after all, an instrument designed to make his Journal seem worth reading. We can claim an intertextual input from Lermontov 4, too, in that, having read Pechorin's Journal, the Narrator, Lermontov 3, may have been influenced by it stylistically, and even ideologically (e.g. the paradoxical content of the Foreword). In the same way, Lermontov 4 may be held to have indirectly motivated the writing of the Preface since it is misreadings of his character by the public which the Preface seeks to correct. But whereas it is clear that Lermontov 3 wrote the Foreword, it is not clear whether the Preface should be regarded as emanating from Lermontov 1 or from Lermontov 2. If it is regarded as an integral part of the text, however, it must be regarded as authored by Lermontov 2; if not, Lermontov 1. Turner's view is that, faced with the negative response which the first edition of *A Hero of Our Time* received, Lermontov 1 could have taken a number of corrective measures ranging from polemical engagements with his critics to a sequel to the novel. By writing a preface instead of a sequel Lermontov 1 seeks to modify the reader's understanding of Lermontov 2, Lermontov 3 and Lermontov 4 by declaring that the whole work should not be taken literally. Whether or not Lermontov 1 had a right to interfere with the reception of the novel in this way, Turner is certain that the Preface should not be treated as an integral part of the novel for the simple reason that it emanates from Lermontov 1, the real Lermontov, who lives and breathes and reacts to adverse criticism, and not from Lermontov 2, the creator of the novel. There are problems with this judgment. As Turner says, Lermontov could have written a sequel to his novel, and, since such a possibility is sustained by the fact that Lermontov 3 claims to have 'another thick note-book' which will be some day '...put before the public' (76) such a work could easily have been represented as, not merely a 'sequel', but as an integral part of *A Hero of Our Time*, the publication of which had merely been delayed for 'a number of important reasons' (76). Clearly then the novel is by definition unfinished: there could be more than there is; problematic readings could be clarified by knowing more about Pechorin, and, under these conditions, it could be argued, intervention by Preface, though unorthodox, is aesthetically justified by the unorthodox epistemic status of the novel as a whole. It is an inherently open-ended and supplementable text.[1]

Although Turner makes comparisons between Preface and Foreword in terms of style and content (noting, for instance, that though irony is mentioned in both texts, it becomes thematically dominant only in the Preface) a more detailed study of the intertextual relationship between the two documents may be found in Krupyshev's article (1989: 63-6). Krupyshev notes that Lermontov 3 (to continue Turner's convention) has an essentially sentimentalist or pre-romantic voice in the Foreword. He puts a high premium on confession as an end in itself, citing Rousseau, though critically. This is the voice of a Karamzinian, drawn to didacticism, who stresses the moral value of publishing the Journal and hopes to be of use to society by so doing. As Krupyshev observes, such views were already passé by Lermontov's day. Lermontov must have known this and could therefore only have been offering them to his public ironically or parodically. The irony, however, was not seen by the readership of the first edition of *A Hero of Our Time* and so Lermontov 1 was forced to add a corrective preface, making clear that Lermontov 3 was not to be taken literally. The two introductions reflect two literary traditions, according to Krupyshev, the Foreword suggesting Karamzinian didacticism, and the Preface the more modern or contemporary ironical view; both, however, are inscribed into the structure of the whole novel.

However, though Krupyshev's argument clearly shows that the Preface must be read with reference to the Foreword, it still does not answer conclusively why Lermontov produced it nor the question of its legitimacy as an integral part of the novel. The Preface does not, in fact, engage with the content of the Foreword in the sense of amplifying it or making it more explicit, but rather as an instruction on how it should be read. Since in the course of a text writers instruct their readers on how to read in many and varied ways it could be argued that in the Preface Lermontov is simply performing this function in a rather unusual way and that it should therefore be regarded as a belated but legitimate intervention by Lermontov 2. (One such intervention may be allowable, but no more!) Reasons of symmetry also make it legitimate for Lermontov 2 to intervene *post factum*: the Journal has an introduction, but the travel notes do not. By adding his Preface Lermontov is creating a symmetry and improving the structure of the whole novel. The hand which improves the structure of the novel is that of Lermontov 2.[2]

Krupyshev notes that the Preface proceeds by thesis and antithesis: 'The Preface is the first and also the last thing in a book' (19); it explains or defends; despite these functions, the reader 'doesn't bother to read the Preface' (19). He sees stylistic affinities between this type of dichotomous formulation and the opening lines of the stories: 'I had...one small portmanteau half-filled with travel notes...Luckily for you most of them have been lost...' (21); '...I travelled...through the Terek and Daryal gorges...But I won't burden you with descriptions...' (62); (and in the Foreword) 'Not long ago I heard that Pechorin had died...I was delighted...' (75 [Krupyshev, 1989: 64]). Such antitheses deceive lectorial expectation and produce a kind of estrangement which forces the reader to be constantly prepared for something new. However these binaries do not occur just at the opening of individual sections of the novel; they can be found throughout, and at other levels than the simply linguistic or stylistic. We find antithetical binaries articulating whole philosophical themes, as in *The Fatalist*: 'If predestination really exists, why have we been given free-will and reason?' (175); or the notion of the 'innocent deception' which sets the tone for the foreword (75).

As I have suggested earlier in this study, *The Fatalist* itself is based on a concessive binary (didn't fire the first time but fired the second) while the corrective or competitive binaries in the form of quips exchanged by Pechorin with Grushnitsky and Werner ('...je haïs les hommes...Je méprise les femmes...[96-7]; '...one fine day...one foul evening...' [101]) illustrate very well the organic or closed structure of this trope. The second element has the form of a conclusion. The eavesdropping or spying device has the same form, laid bare by the ondine in *Taman* ('You saw...you'll tell...'[88]).

Some of these binaries may have logical force but, on the whole, as my treatment of *The Fatalist* implies, their value is rhetorical and rests less on the logical necessity of the second element than on its elegance and appropriateness to the first, irrespective of whether that appropriateness lies in its opposition to or completion of the first element. In this way these binaries and pairings function very much like rhymes, which again are effective on rhetorical and stylistic criteria rather than on logical ones. And, since Lermontov was a poet, it is not surprising that he would have given prominence to devices of formal correspondence in other areas of literary endeavour. Like rhyming pairs the antitheses of the introductions follow one another in resonant parataxis and the reader is drawn along as much by this metrical progression as by the logic of what is said. On this basis, then, we might conclude that the Preface is part of the whole book; figuratively speaking it rhymes with the Foreword and its integral participation in the novel is demonstrated as much formally as ideologically.

There is no doubt, however, that both introductions serve to draw the reader out beyond the concerns of the novel and into the public domain of reading. Todd believes that his decision to publish private notes turns the Narrator into 'another vicious member of society' (146) and it may be that from this point of view he turns out to be a not too admirable member of 'the reading public' which, as Todd says, appears to be a catch-all term for everybody involved in the literary process in Russia whatever the nature of their function (Todd, 1986: 145). Of all the characters in the novel the Narrator is the one most likely to elude moral scrutiny, for, since we ourselves as readers wish to find out what is in the Journal, we must entertain the same sort of ambivalence to him as might readers of a modern tabloid to the reporter who has brought them a prurient story about someone's private life. The opportunism of the Narrator has, however, been there all along and is clearly evident when, having got his story out of Maxim, he ceases to listen to him and by the beginning of *Maxim Maximych* has begun to find him distinctly tedious. With his 'Bela' story to write up he is on the way to making up the deficit of the lost travel notes and need not therefore 'burden' himself, any more than us with 'descriptions of mountains...depictions of scenery...' (62). Lermontov 3 is a publicist and this is what distinguishes him both from Lermontov 4 and from Lermontov 1. He has, unlike Pechorin, a clear readership in mind, one, moreover, with expectations about the Caucasus.

Although Eikhenbaum may be right in claiming that the travel notes drive and motivate the novel, it is, beyond this, the Narrator's tenacious desire to publish (at any price – even another man's work) which controls and shapes the book itself. In a conventional realist Russian novel this process (Lermontov 1's desire to see his novel published) is something assumed by the reader to lie outside the fiction: we take it for granted that an author has wanted and actively sought for the publication of his work. In *A Hero of Our Time*, by contrast, this·dynamic of publication implicit in the existence of every novel is laid bare, by personifying it as a character in the novel itself. The two imperatives of the writer, to create and to publish, appear in *A Hero of Our Time* as distinct characters: Lermontov 4 and Lermontov 3, Pechorin and the Narrator. Because they are separate, each is in deficit where the other is in surplus: the Narrator has a thirst for publicity but, at the beginning of the novel nothing to publish; Pechorin has material written, but no desire to publish. Under these conditions it is hard not to see Maxim Maximych as representing a reading public incapable of understanding or (in carrying round with him an unread Pechorin's Journal) ignorant of the literature available to it. He nevertheless provides the raw material from which literature is made, albeit unwittingly (*Bela* and *Maxim Maximych*).

Perhaps the most remarkable rhyme in this context is that between Maxim in *Bela* and the 'country bumpkin' in the Preface and it is hard not to conclude from the similarities that Lermontov was attempting to mark the significance of the former by means of the latter. In the Preface the eavesdropper, through ignorance of diplomatic protocol, wrongly attributes something subversive to the apparently amicable conversation of two diplomats representing hostile powers. Maxim's mistake when overhearing Kazbich and Azamat is of a subtler order. He perfectly understands the nature and context of their exchange, and, had he not divulged what he overheard there would be no grounds for challenging his judgment. However, by divulging what he has overheard to Pechorin he demonstrates that he has no grasp of the malign potential which such information might have in the mind of Pechorin.

Unlike the country bumpkin in the Preface Maxim is not inherently stupid or ignorant. It is only the blinding presence of Pechorin which casts him into the dark penumbra of confusion and misprision. Pechorin's role in probing the weaknesses and foibles of characters with whom he comes into contact is clearly as important a feature of the novel as the psychology of Pechorin himself. The Preface seems to suggest that for Lermontov 1, writing shortly before his death, the former was indeed the role which he most valued in his hero. Subsequent criticism, however, has steadily moved away from this socially interactive concept of Pechorin in the direction of an ever greater engagement with his complex psychology. Time itself has embedded the Preface into the body of the fiction, for the sensitivity of Lermontov to his public is, for modern readers, totally merged into the chronotope of the novel and inextricably bound to the publicistic concerns of the fictitious Narrator. The modern reader engages with the novel from perspectives undreamt of by Lermontov, or, put another way, the novel continues to invite and reward new critical approaches, a confirmation of the legitimacy of its place as one of the classics of Russian literature.

Notes

1. As George Hyde puts it: '...the novel is not a finished work but a kind of d.i.y. kit which must be assembled each time anew by the reader' (Hyde, 1977: 100).

2. Eikhenbaum notes that medial introductions were not uncommon in fictional works in Lermontov's day: he sees them as a device designed to retard lectorial progress through the text, though, in *A Hero of Our Time* it is more properly a separating device, which takes the reader out of the travel note text and momentarily holds him in a quite separate textual domain, a kind of decompression chamber before he enters the journal proper (Eikhenbaum, 1981: 167).

Bibliography

Primary Sources

M.Iu. Lermontov, *Sobranie sochinenii v chetyrekh tomakh*, E. Zhezlova et al. (eds) (Izdatel'stvo khudozhestvennaia literatura: Moscow, 1965).

Some English Translations

Mikhail Lermontov, *A Hero of Our Time*, translated by Martin Parker; revised and edited by Neil Cornwell (Everyman, J.M. Dent: London 1995; originally published by Progress Publishers, 1947).

Mikhail Lermontov, *A Hero of our Time*, translated by Vladimir Nabokov in collaboration with Dmitri Nabokov (World's Classics: Oxford, 1984; first published by Doubleday and Company, 1958).

Mikhail Yurevich Lermontov, *A Hero of Our Time*, translated by Philip Longworth (The New English Library, 1964; first published by The New English Library, 1962).

M.Yu. Lermontov, *A Hero of Our Time*, translated by Paul Foote (Penguin Books: Harmondsworth, 1966).

Secondary Sources

Aizlewood, Robin, '*Geroi nashego vremeni* as Emblematic Prose Text' in *Pushkin to Palisandriia: Essays on the Russian Novel in Honor of Richard Freeborn*, Arnold McMillin (ed.) (St Martin's Press: New York, 1990) 39-51.

Andrew, Joe, *Writers and Society During the Rise of Russian Realism* (Macmillan: London and Basingstoke, 1980).

——*Women in Russian Literature: 1780-1863* (The Macmillan Press: Basingstoke, 1988).

——'The Blind Will See: Narrative and Gender in *Taman*'; *Russian Literature*, XXXI (1992) 449-76.

Andronikov, I.L, Notes to *Kavkazets* in M.Yu. Lermontov, *Sobranie sochinenii v chetyrekh tomakh*, Khudozhestvennaia literatura, Moscow, 1965, IV, 456.

Annensky, Innokenty, 'Innokenty Annensky on Mikhail Lermontov' in *The Complection of Russian Literature*, Andrew Field (ed.) (Allen Lane: London, 1971) 57-62.

Arian, I, 'Some Aspects of Lermontov's *A Hero of Our Time*', *Forum for Modern Language Studies*, IV, 1 (1968) 22-32.

Asmus, V, 'Krug idei Lermontova' *Literaturnoe nasledstvo*, XLIII-IV (1941) 83-128.

Austin, Paul M., 'New Light on Lermontov's *Bela*', *Russian Language Journal*, XL, 136-7 (1986) 161-5.

Axelrod, M.R., 'The Psychoanalytic Notion of Weltschmerz in Mikhail Lermontov and *A Hero of Our Time*', *Literature and Psychology*, XXXIX, 1-2 (1993) 112-20.

Bagby, Lewis, 'Narrative Double-Voicing in Lermontov's *A Hero of Our Time*', *Slavic and East European Journal*, XXII, 3 (1978) 265-86

Barratt, Andrew and A.D.P. Briggs, *A Wicked Irony: The Rhetoric of Lermontov's 'A Hero of Our Time'* (Bristol Classical Press: Bristol, 1989).

Belinsky, V.G., 'Geroi nashego vremeni. Sochinenie M. Lermontova' in V.G. Belinsky, *Polnoe sobranie sochinenii*, IV (*Stat'i i retsenzii 1840-1*), N.F. Bel'chikov et al. (eds) (Izdatel'stvo Akademii Nauk: Moscow, 1954) 145-6; 173-5; 193-270.

Belov, S.V. 'Dostoevskii i Lermontov' in *Russkaia literatura XIX v.: Voprosy siuzheta i kompozitsii* (Gorkovskii gos. institut: Gorkii, 1975) 128-33.

Blagoi, D.D., *Ot Pushkina do Maiakovskogo: Zakonomernosti razvitiia russkoi literatury XIX – nachala XX veki* (Izd. ak. nauk SSSR: Moscow) 1968.

Bonamour, Jean, 'Naissance d'un roman: remarques sur le cas d'*Un héros de notre temps*', *Cahiers du monde Russe et Soviétique* XXVII 3-4 (1987) 403-10.

Boyd, A.F., *Aspects of the Russian Novel* (Chatto and Windus: London, 1972).

Brown, William Edward, *A History of Russian Literature of the Romantic Period*, IV, (Ardis: Ann Arbor, 1986).

Calder, Angus, *Russia Discovered: Nineteenth-century Fiction from Pushkin to Chekhov* (Heinemann: London, 1976).

Chances, Ellen, *Conformity's Children: An Approach to the Superfluous Man in Russian literature* (Slavica: Columbus, Ohio, 1978).

Chicherin, A.V., *Ocherki po istorii russkogo literaturnogo stilia* (Khudozhestvennaia literatura: Moscow, 1977) 105-6.

Cornwell, Neil, Introduction to Mikhail Lermontov, *A Hero of Our Time*, translated by Martin Parker, revised and edited by Neil Cornwell (Everyman: London, 1995) xii-xx.

D'iakanova, Nina, 'Byron and Lermontov: Notes on Pechorin's "Journal"' in *Lord Byron and His Contemporaries: Essays from the Sixth International Byron Seminar*, Charles E. Robinson (ed) (University of Delaware Press: London and Toronto, 1982) 144-65.

Durylin, S., *'Geroi nashego vremeni' M.Yu. Lermontova* (Uchebno-pedagogicheskoe izdatel'stvo narkomprosa RSFSR: Moscow, 1940).

Dynnik, Aleksandr, *Russkaia literatura pervoi poloviny XIX veka: obzor i analiz* (Russkaia kniga: New York, 1932).

Eagle, Herbert, 'Lermontov's "Play" with Romantic Genre Expectations in *A Hero of Our Time*', *Russian Literature Tri-Quarterly*, 10, Fall (1994): 'The Golden Age', 299-315.

Efremov, V., *Ocherki po istorii russkoi literatury XIX veka* (Izdanie knizhnego magazina Viktor Kamkin: Washington, 1966).

Eikhenbaum, B.M., '*Geroi nashego vremeni*'in B.M. Eikhenbaum, *Stat'i o Lermontove* (Izdatel'stvo Akademii nauk: Leningrad, 1961) 221-85.

——*Lermontov: A Study in Literary-Historical Evolution*, translated by Ray Parrott and Harry Weber (Ardis: Ann Arbor, 1981).

Fedders, G.Iu., *Evoliutsiia tipa 'strannogo cheloveka' u Lermontova po ego dramaticheskim proizvedeniiam, poemam i romanu 'Geroi nashego vremeni'* (Tipo-lit V.K. Melenevskogo: Nezhin, 1914).

Fedoseenko, N.G., 'Roman M.Yu. Lermontova, *Geroi nashego vremeni* i traditsii romanticheskoi poemy', *Vestnik Leningradskogo Universiteta: Seriia istorii iazyka i literatury*, IV, October (1989) 60-6.

Field, Andrew ed., *The Complection of Russian Literature* (Allen Lane: London, 1971) 57-62

Fokht, U.R, Lermontov entry in *Istoriia russkoi literatury*, II (Literatura pervoi poloviny XIX veka), ed. A.M. Lavretsky et al. (Izdatel'stvo Akademii nauk: Moscow-Leningrad, 1963) 530-90.

——*Lermontov: Logika tvorchestva* (Nauka: Moscow, 1975).

France, Peter, 'Western European Civilization and its Mountain Frontiers (1750-1850)', *History of European Ideas*, VI, 3 (1985) 297-310.

Freeborn, Richard, *The Rise of the Russian Novel: Studies in the Russian Novel from 'Eugene Onegin' to 'War and Peace'* (Cambridge University Press: Cambridge, 1973).

Gadzhiev, Agil', *Kavkaz v russkoi literature pervoi poloviny XIX veka* (Yazyki: Baku, 1982).

Garrard, John G., 'Old Wine in New Bottles: The Legacy of Lermontov' in *Poetica Slavica: Studies in Honor of Zbigniev Folejeuski*, J. Douglas Clayton (ed.) (University of Ottawa Press: Ottawa, 1981) 41-52.

——*Mikhail Lermontov* (Twayne Publishers: Boston, 1982).

Gavin, W.G., 'Heroes and Deconstruction: Lermontov's *A Hero of Our Time*', *Studies in Soviet Thought*, XXXIV, 4 (1987) 255-66.

Gershtein, E, *'Geroi nashego vremeni' M.Yu Lermontova* (Khudozhestvennaia literatura: Moscow, 1976).

Gifford, Henry, *A Hero of His Time: A Theme in Russian Literature* (Edward Arnold: London, 1950).

Gilroy, Marie, *The Ironic Vision of Lermontov's 'A Hero of Our Time'* (Birmingham Slavonic Monographs 19: University of Birmingham: Birmingham, 1989).

Gorelov, A.E., *Ocherki o russkikh pisateliakh* (Sovetskii pisatel': Leningrad, 1964)

Gorelov, I.N., 'Na chto obidelsia Maksim Maksimych? Zametki o kul'ture obshcheniia', *Russkaia rech': Nauchno-populiarnyi zhurnal*, IV, July-August (1984) 77-80.

Goscilo, Helena, 'Lermontov's Debt to Lavater and Gall', *Slavonic and East European Review*, LIX,4 (1981) 500-15.

——'The First Pechorin en route to a Hero': Lermontov's *Princess Ligovskaia'*, *Russian Literature*, XI (1982) 129-62.

Gregg, Richard, 'The Cooling of Pechorin: The Skull beneath the Skin', *Slavic Review*, XLIII, 3, Fall (1984) 387-98.

Grigoryan, K.N., *Lermontov i ego roman 'Geroi nashego vremeni'* (Nauka: Leningrad, 1975).

Grossman, Leonid, 'Lermontov i kul'tury vostoka' in *Literaturnoe nasledstvo*, 43-4, *M.Iu Lermontov* I, P.I. Lebedev (ed.) (Izdatel'stvo Akademii nauk SSSR: Moscow, 1941) 675-744.

Hansen-Löve, A., 'Pečorin als Frau und Pferd und andere zu Lermontovs *Geroj našego vremeni*' *Russian Literature*, XXXI (1992) 491-544 and XXXIII (1993) 413-70.

Harkins, William E., afterword to Mikhail Yurevich Lermontov, *A Hero of Our Time*, translated by Philip Longworth (Signet Classics: New York, 1964) 193-206.

Heldt, Barbara, *Terrible Perfection: Women and Russian Literature* (Indiana University Press: Bloomington and Indianapolis, 1987).

Hingley, Ronald, *Russian Writers and Society 1825-1904* (Weidenfeld and Nicolson: London, 1964).

Hokanson, Katya, 'Literary Imperialism, *Narodnost'* and Pushkin's Invention of the Caucasus', *Russian Review*, LIII, 3 (1994) 336-52.

Hyde, George, *Vladimir Nabokov: America's Russian Novelist* (Marion Boyars, London, 1977).

——'Translation as Criticism: Vladimir Nabokov's *A Hero of Our Time*' in *Mikhail Lermontov: Commemorative Essays*, A.D.P. Briggs (ed.) (Birmingham Modern Languages Publications: Birmingham, 1992) 67-77.

Ivanov-Razumnik, *Istoriia russkoi obshchestvennoi mysli*, I (St Petersburg, 1911, repr. Mouton: The Hague, 1969).

Kartashova, I.V., 'Romantizm M.Iu. Lermontova' in N.A. Guliaev, ed. *Russkii romantizm* (Vysshaia shkola: Moscow, 1974) 117-38.

Kelly, Laurence, *Lermontov: Tragedy in the Caucasus* (Constable: London, 1977).

Kesler, R.L., 'Fate and Narrative Structure in Lermontov's *A Hero of Our Time*', *Texas Studies in Literature and Language*, XXXII, 4 (1990) 485-505.

Kirpotin, V., *Vershiny: Pushkin, Lermontov, Nekrasov* (Khudozhhestvennaia literatura: Moscow, 1970).

Kornblatt, Judith Deutsch, *The Cossack Hero in Russian Literature: A Study in Cultural Mythology* (University of Wisconsin Press: Madison, Wisconsin, 1992).

Krupyshev, A.M., 'O predisloviiakh v romane M.Yu. Lermontova *Geroi nashego vremeni*', *Filologicheskie nauki*, VI (1989), 63-6.

Lavrin, J, *Russian Writers: Their Lives and Literature* (D. Van Nostrand: New York, 1954).

——*Lermontov* (Bowes and Bowes: London, 1959).

——*A Panorama of Russian Literature* (University of London Press: London, 1973).

Layton, Susan, *Russian Literature and Empire: Conquest of the Caucasus from Pushkin to Tolstoy* (Cambridge University Press: Cambridge, 1994).

Lotman, Jurij, *The Structure of the Artistic Text*, translated by Ronald Vroon (Michigan Slavic Contributions No. 7: University of Michigan, Ann Arbor, 1977).

——'Problema vostoka i zapada v tvorchestve pozdnego Lermontova' in *Lermontovsii sbornik*, I.S. Chistova (ed.) (Nauka: Leningrad, 1985) 5-22.

Manuilov, V.A., *Roman M.Yu. Lermontova 'Geroi nashego vremeni': kommentarii, posobie dlia uchitelia* (Prosveshchenie: Leningrad, 1975).

——'Mozhno li nazvat' Pechorina soznatel'nym pobornikom zla?' in *Problemy teorii i istorii literatury: Sbornik statei posviashchennyi pamiati Prof. A.N. Sokolova*, V.I. Kuleshov (ed.) (Moscow, 1977) 219-25.

Markovich, V.M., 'O znachenii nezavershennosti v proze Lermontova', *Russian Literature*, XXXIII (1993) 471-94.

Marsh, Cynthia, 'Lermontov and the Romantic Tradition: The Function of Landscape in *A Hero of Our Time*', *The Slavonic and East European Review*, LXVI, 1 (1988) 35-46.

Merezhkovsky, D.S., *Izbrannye stat'i*, ed. Karl Eimermacher et al., (Wilhelm Fink Verlag: Munich, 1972).

Mersereau, John, Jr, 'The Fatalist as a Keystone of *A Hero of Our Time*', *The Slavic and East European Journal*, XLV (1960) 137-46.

——*Mikhail Lermontov* (South Illinois University Press: Carbondale, 1962).

——*Russian Romantic Fiction* (Ardis: Ann Arbor, 1983).

Meyer, Priscilla, 'Lermontov's Reading of Pushkin: *The Tales of Belkin* and *A Hero of Our Time*' in *The Golden Age of Russian Literature and Thought: Selected Papers from the Fourth World Congress of Soviet and East European Studies*, Derek Offord (ed.) (St Martin's Press: New York, and Macmillan, Basingstoke,1992) 58-75.

Meyers, Jeffrey, 'The Duel in Fiction', *The North Dakota Quarterly*, LI, 4, (1993) 129-50.

Miller, Tsetsiliia, 'Lermontov Reads *Eugene Onegin*', *Russian Review*, LIII, 1 (1994) 59-66.

Milner-Gulland, Robin, 'Heroes of Their Time: Form and Idea in Buchner's *Danton's Death* and Lermontov's *A Hero of Our Time*', in *The Idea of Freedom: Essays in Honour of Isaiah Berlin*, Alan Ryan (ed.) (Oxford University Press: Oxford, 1979) 115-37.

Nabokov, Vladimir, translator's foreword in Mikhail Lermontov, *A Hero of Our Time*, translated by Vladimir and Dmitri Nabokov (The World's Classics: Oxford, 1984) vii-xix.

Nakhapetov, B.A., 'Obraz doktora Vernera iz romana M.Yu. Lermontova *Geroi nashego vremeni* kak ob"ekt psikhologicheskogo eksperimentirovaniia', *Voprosy psikhologii*, II (1990) 91-7.

Odinokov, V.G., *Problemy poetiki i tipologii russkogo romana XIX veka* (Nauka: Novosibirsk, 1971).

Ovsyaniko-Kulikovsky, D.N., *Istoriia russkoi literatury XIX v.*, II (Slavistic Printings and Reprintings, Mouton: The Hague and Paris, 1969).

Peace, R.A., 'The Role of *Taman'* in Lermontov's *Geroy nashego vremeni*', *The Slavonic and East European Review*, XLV (1967). 12-29.

Pozov, A., *Metafizika Lermontova* (Dr A. Posoff: Madrid, 1975).

Price, Richard H. et al., *Principles of Psychology* (Holt, Rinehart and Winton: New York, 1982).

Reeve, F.D., *The Russian Novel* (McGraw-Hill: New York, 1966).

Reid, R., 'Eavesdropping in *A Hero of Our Time*', *New Zealand Slavonic Journal*, I, (1977) 13-22.

——'The Critical Uses of Translation: Lermontov's *A Hero of Our Time*', *Essays in Poetics* XI, 2, (1986) 55-90.

Richards, D.J., Introduction to M.Yu.Lermontov, *Geroi nashego vremeni* (Bristol Classical Press: London, 1994) vii-xxvi, first published 1965.

——'Lermontov: *A Hero of Our Time*' in *The Voice of A Giant*, Roger Cockrell and David Richards (eds) (University of Exeter: Exeter, 1985) 15-25.

Ripp, Victor, '*A Hero of Our Time* and the Historicism of the 1830s: The Problem of the Whole and the Parts', *Modern Language Notes*, XCII, 2 (1977) 169-86.

Rosenshield, Gary, 'Fatalism in *A Hero of Our Time*: Cause or Commonplace?' in *The Supernatural in Slavic and Baltic Literature: Essays in Honor of Victor Terras*, Amy Mandelker and Roberta Reeder (eds)(Slavica: Columbus, Ohio, 1988) 83-101.

Rowe, Eleanor, 'Pushkin, Lermontov and Hamlet', *Texas Studies in Literature and Language*, XVII (1975) 337-47.

Rowe, W.W., *Nabokov and Others: Patterns in Russian Literature* (Ardis: Ann Arbor, Michigan, 1979).

Sasaki, Teruhiro, 'Razdvoenie geroev Lermontova i ego psikhologicheskoe vliianie na sub"ektivizm P.L. Lavrova', *Russian Literature*, XXXIII (1993) 495-504.

Schmid, Wolf, 'O novatorstve lermontovskogo psikhologizma', *Russian Literature*, XXXIV (1993) 59-74.

Scotto, Peter, 'Prisoners of the Caucasus: Ideologies of Imperialism in Lermontov's *Bela*', *PMLA*, CVII, 2 (1992) 246-60.

Sengupta, Nivedita, 'An Introduction to Lermontov's *A Hero of Our Time*' in *Studies in Russian Literature*, J.V. Paul (ed.) (Central Institute of English and Foreign Languages: Hyderabad, 1984) 19-27.

Shevyryov, S.P., '*Geroi nashego vremeni*. Sochineniia M. Lermontova' in *Russkaia literatura XIX v.: Khrestomatiia kriticheskikh materialov* (Vysshaia shkola: Moscow, 1967) 300-2.

Simpson, Mark S., *The Officer in Nineteenth-Century Russian Literature* (University Press of America: Washington, 1981).

Slonim, M., *The Epic of Russian Literature from Its Inception through Tolstoy* (Oxford University Press: New York, 1950).

Sokolov, A.N., *Ot romantizma k realizmu* (Izd. Moskovskogo universiteta: Moscow, 1957).

——*Istoriia russkoi literatury XIX veka*, I (Izd. Moskovskogo universiteta: Moscow, 1965).

Sollertinsky, E.E., *Russkii realisticheskii roman pervoi poloviny XIX veka: Problemy zhanra* (Volog. gos. ped. institut: Vologda, 1973).

Spector, Ivar, *The Golden Age of Russian Literature* (Caxton Printers: Caldwell, Idaho, 1952).

Terras, Victor, *A History of Russian Literature* (Yale University Press: New Haven and London, 1991).

Todd Mills III, William, *Fiction and Society in the Age of Pushkin: Ideology, Institutions and Narrative* (Harvard University Press: Cambridge, Mass., 1986).

Turner, Charles Edward, *Studies in Russian Literature* (Sampson Low: London, 1882).

Turner, C.J.G., *Pechorin: An Essay on Lermontov's 'Hero of Our Time'* (Birmingham Slavonic Monographs: Birmingham, 1978).

Udodov, B.T., '*Geroi nashego vremeni*' in *Lermontovskaia Entsiklopediia*, V.A. Manuilov (ed.) (Sovetskaia entsiklopediia: Moscow, 1981) 101-11.

Usok, I.E., '*Geroi nashego vremeni*' in *M.Yu. Lermontov v shkole* (Prosveshchenie: Moscow, 1976) 122-40.

——'Istoricheskaia sud'ba naslediia M.Iu. Lermontova' in *Vremia i sud'by russkikh pisatelei* (Nauka: Moscow, 1981) 49-94.

Van der Eng, Jan, 'The Character of Maksim Maksimyč', *Russian Literature*, XXXIV (1993) 21-36.

Van Holk, André, 'Character and Text Linguistics. On the Deep Structure of Pechorin' in *Filologia e letteratura nei paesi slavi. Studi in onore di Sante Graciotti*, G.B. Bercoff et al. (eds) (Rome, 1990) 891-903.

——'O glubinnoi strukture Pechorina', *Russian Literature* XXXI (1992) 545-54.

Vatsuro, V., 'Chuzhoe "Ia" v lermontovskom tvorchestve', *Russian Literature*, XXXIII (1993) 505-20.

Vinogradov, I., 'Filosovskii roman Lermontova' in D. Ustiuzhanin, ed., *Russkaia klassicheskaia literatura: razbory i analizy* (Prosveshchenie: Moscow, 1969) 156-85.

Vinogradov, V., 'Stil' prozy Lermontova' in *Literaturnoe nasledstvo*, 43-4, *M.Iu Lermontov* I, P.I. Lebedev (ed.) (Izdatel'stvo Akademii nauk SSSR: Moscow, 1941) 518-628.

Vishevsky, Anatoly, 'Demonic Games or the Hidden Plot of Mixail Lermontov's *Knjažna Meri*', *Wiener Slawistischer Almanach*, XXVII (1991) 55-71.

Waliszewski, K., *A History of Russian Literature* (Heinemann: London, 1900).

Warner, Nicholas O., 'The Footnote as Literary Genre: Nabokov's Commentaries to Lermontov and Pushkin', *The Slavic and East European Journal*, XXX, 2 (1986) 167-82.

Waszink, Paul, 'Artist, Writer and Peircean Interpretant: Some Observations on Nineteenth-Century Art and Literature', *Zeitschrift für Slavische Philologie*, L, 2 (1990) 305-29.

Wilden, Anthony, *The Rules Are No Game: The Strategy of Communication* (Routledge and Kegan Paul: London and New York, 1987).

Zholkovsky, A., 'Semiotika *Tamani*' in *Sbornik statei k 70-letiiu Iu.M. Lotmana*, A. Mal'ts (ed.) (Tartu University: Tartu, 1992) 248-56.

Zhuravleva, A.I., 'Pechorin in pechorinstvo v 1840-1850e gody (zhizn' literaturnogo obraza v istorii)', *Vestnik moskovskogo universiteta*, ser. IX (Filologiia) 6 (1991) 3-11.

Second Edition Addenda

Bagby, Lewis, 'Inscription in *Fatalist*', *Romantic Russia*, II (1998) 35-47.

Golstein, Vladimir, *Lermontov's Narratives of Heroism* (Northwestern University Press: Evanston, Illinois, 1998).

Index